THE
BIG
BOOK
of
TOOLS

for Collaborative Teams

in a PLC at Work®

WILLIAM M. FERRITER

Solution Tree | Press

a division of
Solution Tree

555 North Morton Street
Bloomington, IN 47404
800.733.6786 (toll free) / 812.336.7700
FAX: 812.336.7790

email: info@SolutionTree.com
SolutionTree.com

Visit **go.SolutionTree.com/PLCbooks** to download the free reproducibles in this book.

Visit **go.SolutionTree.com/PLCbooks/BBTCT** and enter the unique access code found on the inside front cover to access the exclusive online reproducibles in this book.

Printed in the United States of America

Library of Congress Cataloging-in-Publication Data

Names: Ferriter, William M., author.
Title: The big book of tools for collaborative teams in a PLC at work /
    William M. Ferriter.
Description: Bloomington, IN : Solution Tree Press, [2020] | Includes
    bibliographical references and index.
Identifiers: LCCN 2019044839 (print) | LCCN 2019044840 (ebook) | ISBN
    9781947604858 (paperback) | ISBN 9781947604865 (ebook)
Subjects: LCSH: Teaching teams. | Teachers--In-service training. | School
    improvement programs.
Classification: LCC LB1029.T4 F47 2020 (print) | LCC LB1029.T4 (ebook) |
    DDC 371.14/8--dc23
LC record available at https://lccn.loc.gov/2019044839
LC ebook record available at https://lccn.loc.gov/2019044840

Solution Tree
Jeffrey C. Jones, CEO
Edmund M. Ackerman, President

Solution Tree Press
President and Publisher: Douglas M. Rife
Associate Publisher: Sarah Payne-Mills
Art Director: Rian Anderson
Managing Production Editor: Kendra Slayton
Production Editor: Miranda Addonizio
Content Development Specialist: Amy Rubenstein
Copy Editor: Mark Hain
Proofreader: Jessi Finn
Cover Designer: Rian Anderson
Editorial Assistants: Sarah Ludwig and Elijah Oates

Acknowledgments

This book is dedicated to all teachers who are committed to studying their practice in service of student learning. My hope is that these tools will provide your team with the structures that you need in order to make higher levels of learning for *all* a doable reality.

Solution Tree Press would like to thank the following reviewers:

Drake Bailey
Social Studies Teacher
Bondurant-Farrar Middle School
Bondurant, Iowa

Kimberly Calcasola
Assistant Principal
Granby Memorial High School
Granby, Connecticut

Mary Beth Fischer
French Teacher
Kinard Middle School
Fort Collins, Colorado

Cheryl Hermach
Language Arts Teacher
Lafayette High School
Wildwood, Missouri

Brad McCloskey
Principal and Special Education Director
Davis County Middle School
Bloomfield, Iowa

Joseph O'Brien
Assistant Principal
Vernon Hills High School
Lake County, Illinois

Bo Ryan
Principal
Greater Hartford Academy of the
    Arts Middle School
Hartford, Connecticut

Kimberly Ziehl
Assistant Principal
Grady Rasco Middle School
Lake Jackson, Texas

Visit **go.SolutionTree.com/PLCbooks** to download the free reproducibles in this book.

Visit **go.SolutionTree.com/PLCbooks/BBTCT** and enter the unique access code found on the inside front cover to access the exclusive online reproducibles in this book.

Table of Contents

Reproducible pages are in italics.

4   How Will We Respond When Some Students Don't Learn? 149

Five Fundamental Resources for Responding When Some Students Don't Learn

Additional Resources for Responding When Some Students Don't Learn

About the Author

William M. Ferriter is an eighth-grade science teacher in a professional learning community near Raleigh, North Carolina. A National Board Certified Teacher for the past twenty-five years, Bill has designed professional development courses for educators across the United States on topics ranging from establishing professional learning communities and using technology to reimagine learning spaces to integrating meaningful student-involved assessment and feedback opportunities into classroom instruction.

What Bill brings to audiences is practical experience gained through extensive and continuing work with his own professional learning team and students in his classroom. Teachers appreciate the practicality of both his writing and his presentations because they know that his content is being used by a full-time classroom teacher. Every book that he writes and session that he delivers is designed to give participants not just a clear understanding of the *whys* behind the ideas that he is introducing, but tangible examples of how to turn those ideas into classroom and collaborative practices that work.

Bill has had articles published in *Phi Delta Kappan* magazine, the *Journal of Staff Development*, *Educational Leadership*, and *Threshold Magazine*. A contributing author to two assessment anthologies, *The Teacher as Assessment Leader* and *The Principal as Assessment Leader*, he is also coauthor of several Solution Tree titles, including *Teaching the iGeneration*, *Building a Professional Learning Community at Work®*, *Making Teamwork Meaningful*, and *Creating a Culture of Feedback*.

Bill earned a bachelor of science and master of science in elementary education from the State University of New York at Geneseo.

To learn more about Bill's work, visit his blog *The Tempered Radical* (http://blog.williamferriter.com) or follow @plugusin on Twitter.

To book William M. Ferriter for professional development, contact pd@SolutionTree.com.

Introduction

If there is one thing that we know about improving schools, it's that *nothing* has a greater impact on student learning than organizing teachers into collaborative teams committed to studying their practice together. These professional learning teams can do much more than their members can do alone. They act as engines that drive the greater school community. Teachers who study their practice together are more persistent, more likely to set challenging goals for themselves, and more likely to experiment with their instruction than teachers working in isolation (Donohoo, 2017). Studying practice together also builds professional confidence in collaborative teams, leaving teachers convinced that they have the shared capacity to drive meaningful change in their own classrooms. The result: members of collaborative teams are more likely to have a positive impact on *every* student—including those from disadvantaged backgrounds or those who have traditionally struggled in schools. Education researcher John Hattie (2017) calls this *collective teacher efficacy*. In his most recent summary of the work that we do in schools, Hattie (2017) places collective teacher efficacy first in a list of 252 practices ranked in order as having the greatest "potential to considerably accelerate student achievement."

But ask teachers who have ever worked in a Professional Learning Community (PLC) at Work® and they will tell you that studying practice together isn't always as easy as it sounds. The greatest challenge for some learning teams is the energy and effort that studying practice together requires. Identifying essential outcomes, developing unit plans, and creating assessments together takes more time than doing that same work on your own—and it requires negotiation and compromise, something that teachers used to working in isolation are often unprepared for. Collective inquiry around instruction also requires *coordination*. Working interdependently to study practice depends on every member of a team teaching roughly the same content and skills at roughly the same time. If members struggle to keep up—or just plain disagree with shared pacing decisions—collective inquiry around instruction becomes impossible.

Learning teams can also struggle with the interpersonal skills necessary for working interdependently. Assertive members can dominate conversations and decisions, pushing their more measured colleagues away. Different pedagogical viewpoints or professional experiences can cause teachers to openly question the intentions and abilities of their peers. New teachers—or teachers new to their teams—can defer to veteran colleagues, unwilling to challenge well-established social hierarchies in their schools or at their grade levels. Vulnerability and intellectual humility, traits essential to all those interested in learning from their peers, require high levels of trust that teachers used to working alone have never had to develop with one another before. Teams that suffer from these issues fall into uncomfortable and unproductive patterns of participation that limit the overall impact of their work, leading teachers to doubt the overall value of studying their practice together.

Finally, even seasoned learning teams can struggle with the core practices necessary to shift from a focus on teaching to a focus on learning. Unpacking complex objectives into individual learning targets, developing common formative assessments that provide actionable information, and tracking progress by both student and standard are often new behaviors for members of collaborative teams. Learning teams can also have skill gaps in data collection and analysis, finding it difficult to collect, sort, and learn from the results that they are gathering with one another. Lastly, learning teams can find it difficult to integrate timely and directive opportunities for intervention and extension into their instructional plans. Lacking clear processes for what serve as everyday activities on collaborative teams in PLCs can make initial attempts at studying practice together feel inefficient to teachers.

So, what's the best way to work through the challenges that can cause learning teams to stumble? Professional Learning Community at Work expert Richard DuFour (2004) offers a hint when he writes:

> Collaborative conversations call on team members to make public what has traditionally been private—goals, strategies, materials, pacing, questions, concerns, and results. These discussions give every teacher someone to turn to and talk to, and they are explicitly structured to improve the classroom practice of teachers— individually and collectively. Teams must focus their efforts on crucial questions related to learning and generate products that reflect that focus, such as lists of essential outcomes, different kinds of assessment, analyses of student achievement, and strategies for improving results.

Can you spot the key in DuFour's quote? Overcoming the challenges of working as a team depends on discussions that are *explicitly structured to improve classroom practice* and *focused on the generation of products* (DuFour, 2004).

Chances are that your learning team is already generating lots of shared products: unit plans, lists of students in need of remediation, extension activities, and data analysis tools and protocols. And chances are that you *enjoy* generating products with one another. Generating products feels a lot like planning to learning teams, particularly when those same products can be used as part of the daily work of individual teachers. Each useful product that a team generates serves as a tangible reminder that time spent working together is worthwhile. But here is a question worth asking: "Are the work products that your learning team is generating *explicitly structured to improve classroom practice*?"

The Big Book of Tools for Collaborative Teams in a PLC at Work is a collection of resources designed to provide that explicit structure for your learning team. The first chapter provides guidance for beginning work with your learning team. Then, chapters 2 through 5 contain resources organized to mirror the four critical questions of learning in a PLC at Work, as proposed by Richard DuFour, Rebecca DuFour, Robert Eaker, Thomas W. Many, and Mike Mattos (2016).

- **Chapter 1, "Strengthening the Collegial Practices of Learning Teams":** Collaborative teams establish a solid foundation of collegial practices that govern their work. The tools in this chapter are designed to help your team build this foundation. They include templates for establishing norms, building trust, resolving conflict, creating agendas, and monitoring the quality of work that teams are doing together.

- **Chapter 2, "What Do We Want Students to Learn?":** Collaboration that improves the classroom practice of teachers starts with the development of a guaranteed and viable curriculum. The tools in this chapter are designed to help your team develop this curriculum. They include templates for identifying essential standards, communicating expected outcomes to learners, writing SMART goals (Conzemius & O'Neill, 2014), and developing comprehensive plans for units of instruction.

- **Chapter 3, "How Will We Know Students Are Learning?":** Collaboration that improves the classroom practice of teachers also depends on using assessments to collect evidence of the impact that our professional choices are having on learners. The tools in this chapter are designed to build the assessment capacity of your learning team. They include templates for writing common formative assessments; collecting, organizing, and learning from data; turning students into partners in the assessment process; and reflecting on instructional strengths and weaknesses.

- **Chapter 4, "How Will We Respond When Some Students Don't Learn?":** Collaboration that improves the classroom practice of teachers always results in action on behalf of students. The tools in this chapter are designed to help your team integrate interventions for remediation into your instruction. They include templates for tracking student interventions, documenting the common misconceptions identified during a unit of instruction, creating student intervention reports, and reflecting on the effectiveness of individual intervention strategies.

- **Chapter 5, "How Will We Extend Learning When Students Are Already Proficient?":** Collaborative teams recognize that taking action on behalf of students doesn't just refer to providing interventions to students who are struggling to master essential outcomes. It also means extending learning for students who are already proficient with grade-level essentials. The tools in this chapter are designed to strengthen the work that your team does with these "question 4" students. They include templates for planning weekly extensions, increasing the cognitive complexity of existing tasks, and developing tiered lesson plans.

The content included in *The Big Book of Tools for Collaborative Teams in a PLC at Work* is also organized into two separate sections within each chapter: (1) the five fundamentals and (2) additional resources for extending the work of your team. The five fundamentals are the five most important templates in the entire chapter. They are designed to provide explicit structure to core behaviors that your team simply can't live without. For example, readers will find resources for setting norms and for coming to consensus in the five fundamentals for chapter 1 because those behaviors are essential to collaborative success. Additional resources for extending the work of your team are supplementary templates designed to help your team go beyond core behaviors and navigate unique situations. In chapter 1, for instance, those resources include strategies for resolving conflict between colleagues and for evaluating the levels of trust on your learning team. Throughout the text, I have included samples that show the more complex tools filled out so you can get a better idea of how you can use them in your work. You can find these immediately following their corresponding templates.

To collaborate effectively, it's important to have the reproducible tools in this book at the ready. You can visit **go.SolutionTree.com/PLCbooks** to digitally access many of the reproducibles this book offers. However, because *The Big Book of Tools for Collaborative Teams in a PLC at Work* is filled with over one hundred reproducibles, we only offer a portion on this freely accessible landing page. Therefore, on the inside front cover of your book, you will find a unique access code to digitally access *all* reproducibles, including the remaining exclusive reproducibles. These exclusive reproducibles will only be available to those who purchase the book. The code on the inside front cover of your book is unique to your book, and your book alone, and you can only use it once. Visit **go.SolutionTree.com/PLCbooks/BBTCT** to enter your access code. After entering your code, the exclusive reproducibles will then be added to your customer dashboard on the Solution Tree website, allowing you access to the reproducibles at any time. Each reproducible printed in the book indicates which reproducibles are available on **go.SolutionTree.com/PLCbooks** and which will only be available with a unique access code. The reproducibles in this book offer the most complete toolkit that your collaborative team can use to tackle all the many tasks you must accomplish every day, year after year.

While the content included in *The Big Book of Tools for Collaborative Teams in a PLC at Work* is intentionally organized around the four critical questions of learning in a PLC at Work (DuFour et al., 2016), and while those questions are intentionally designed to be answered sequentially as teams work through ongoing cycles of inquiry around their practice, there is no one right way to read this book. If you are new to collaboration, you might choose to read from cover to cover in order to get a better sense of the types of products that you can use to structure collaborative practice. Or you might decide to limit your study to the five fundamentals found in each chapter, knowing that they can become solid starting points for the work that you are doing with your peers. If you have been collaborating for a while, however, turn *The Big Book of Tools for Collaborative Teams in a PLC at Work* into a toolkit that you can draw from on an as-needed basis. Use the table of contents and the description of individual tools at the beginning of each chapter to find specific resources that can address the immediate challenges of your learning team. The resource "Matrix: Identifying Resources Worth Exploring" (pages 8–11), which details the common stages of learning team development and offers specific tool recommendations for each stage, might also be a helpful starting point. You can use it as a checklist to identify the stage of development that your learning team is in and the resources in this book that might be worth exploring first.

Here are a few additional tips that can help you take full advantage of *The Big Book of Tools for Collaborative Teams in a PLC at Work*.

1. **Remember that *meaningfully collaborating around practice* and *filling out worksheets during team meetings* are *not* the same thing:** The resources provided in this text really *are* designed to explicitly structure collaborative work—and teams that use them to target their time together really *will* find that their regular meetings are more productive than ever before. As education consultant Susan K. Sparks (2008) explains in *The Collaborative Teacher*:

   > The most effective teams are clear about the why, what, where, how, and when of their work. . . . Defined roles and responsibilities may seem formal, . . . [but] when the team sees results, members will appreciate its structure: "Our team is focused and organized. We share roles and responsibilities, and we get our work done." (pp. 42–43)

   But don't fall into the trap of thinking that just because you are filling out a ton of worksheets, you are "doing PLCs" right. In fact, if filling out worksheets feels like the primary purpose of your weekly meetings, you are probably doing PLCs all wrong! The tools included in this book aren't designed to keep learning teams busy. Instead, they are designed to encourage your team to engage in systematic reflection about your practice—and systematic reflection is the key to leveraging the power of collective inquiry to improve teaching and learning.

2. **Remember that your team may not currently need some of the tools found in this text:** Readers of *The Big Book of Tools for Collaborative Teams in a PLC at Work* will quickly find that it is exactly as advertised: a comprehensive collection of resources that addresses the full range of collaborative practices that learning teams may have to wrestle with at one point or another in their work together. Some of those practices—setting norms, writing common assessments, planning for intervention and extension—are universal for teams in PLCs at Work. But others—resolving conflict, integrating student self-assessment into instruction, conducting peer observations—are practices that your team may only tackle once or twice during your entire career. Similarly, some of the collaborative practices spotlighted in *The Big Book of Tools for Collaborative Teams in a PLC at Work* will be brand new to your learning team and others will be practices that you have already mastered.

    That means it is better to think of this text as a cookbook full of recipes to explore instead of a to-do list full of tasks to complete. Find the templates that are worth experimenting with right now and skip the ones that aren't. Then, keep *The Big Book of Tools for Collaborative Teams in a PLC at Work* on your professional bookshelf and turn to it for direction the next time that your team has a new challenge to tackle.

3. **Remember that you can modify these tools in order to make them more useful to your learning team:** This book was born from an argument that Richard DuFour, the original architect of the Professional Learning Community at Work process along with Robert Eaker, would make when talking about moving collaborative teams forward: school leaders can use the creation of products to reinforce core learning community behaviors (R. DuFour, personal communication, June 14, 2011). Want teams to work together to determine just what students should know and be able to do? Ask them to generate a list of essential standards for every unit in their required curriculum. Expect teams to develop shared agreements about what mastery looks like in action? Ask them to develop sets of proficiency scales for an upcoming assignment. Working together doesn't improve teaching and learning, DuFour liked to say; *doing the right work together* improves teaching and learning—and specific work products can help teams spend more of their collaborative time doing the right work (personal communication, June 14, 2011).

The tools included in this text, then, lay out one way that teams can start doing the right work together. Need a strategy for setting norms? Not sure what a set of essential standards for each unit should look like? Struggling to organize student learning data in a way that makes sense? The templates in this book might be exactly what you are looking for—and if they are, use them exactly as they are written.

But also recognize that you don't *have* to use these tools exactly as they are written. Like one part of a template but not another? Think you could simplify a resource to make it more approachable for your team? Want to integrate a series of questions or a table from a tool that I have created into a document that your school or district is already using? Then use my ideas as inspiration and modify what you see so that it works better for your collaborative team. That's OK.

4. **Remember to work fast and finish:** Whether you decide to use the templates included in this text exactly as is or to modify them to meet the unique needs of your team or school, remember that you should be able to complete *most* collaborative tasks in no more than sixty minutes. Why? Because schools are busy places, and if a collaborative task takes longer than sixty minutes to complete, you probably won't ever do it again!

   So, adopt a "work fast and finish" attitude when using the tools in this text. Set a timer. Pick a person on your team to be your "reminder," nudging you forward when you get stuck for too long in any single conversation. Strip out parts of individual templates if you need to. Remember that any decision that your team makes or conclusion that your team draws can be revisited and revised in the future, so having the perfect product isn't nearly as important as being willing to work together again next week. Stated another way, remind each other that *being great* at anything—including inquiry around instruction—is just a function of *being good repeatedly* (Smith, 2019). Teams that struggle to complete collaborative tasks in a reasonable amount of time quickly begin to doubt the overall value of working together.

Just know that the primary goal of *The Big Book of Tools for Collaborative Teams in a PLC at Work* is to get the *right resource* into the hands of the *right team* at the *right time*. That's the kind of targeted support necessary for realizing the promise and potential in collective teacher efficacy as a tool for school improvement. When teams develop the skills necessary to engage in ongoing cycles of collective inquiry around the impact that their professional choices are having on student learning, they build confidence in their capacity to be agents of change—and that confidence makes all the difference.

Matrix: Identifying Resources Worth Exploring

Instructions: In "One Step at a Time," collaboration experts Parry Graham and William M. Ferriter (2008) argue that in a PLC at Work, most learning teams move predictably through clear stages of development. In the column marked **Characteristics of This Stage**, use the checkboxes to mark all the statements that accurately describe the current work of your learning team in each stage of team development. Then, use the tasks listed under **Next Steps Worth Taking** to identify a small handful of core collaborative behaviors that your team is ready to embrace. Finally, use the **Resources Worth Exploring** column to locate tools in this book that are explicitly structured to help your team move your collaborative work forward.

Stage of Team Development	Characteristics of This Stage	Next Steps Worth Taking	Resources Worth Exploring
Filling the Time	☐ Teams ask, "What is it exactly that we're supposed to do together?" ☐ Meetings can ramble. ☐ Frustration levels can be high. ☐ Activities are simple and scattered rather than part of a coherent plan for improvement.	☐ Develop a set of norms to govern weekly meetings. ☐ Begin using agendas for every single meeting. ☐ Assign specific roles to individual members of the team based on personal and professional strengths. ☐ Work together to identify three to five essential outcomes for an upcoming unit of study.	• "Tool: Developing Team Norms" (pages 21–23) • "Tool: Establishing Team Roles" (pages 24–26) • "Tool: Learning Team Meeting Notes" (pages 27–28) • "Tool: Team Meeting Evaluation Strips" (page 34) • "Checklist: Identifying Essential Learning Outcomes for a Unit of Study" (page 55) • "Tool: Essential Standards Chart" (pages 76–77) • "Tool: Identifying Important Questions to Study Together" (page 80)

| Sharing Personal Practices

Planning, Planning, Planning | ☐ Teams ask, "What is everyone doing in their classrooms?" or "How can we help each other and lighten our workload?"
☐ Teamwork focuses on sharing instructional practices or resources.
☐ Less experienced colleagues benefit from the planning expertise of colleagues.
☐ Team members delegate planning responsibilities, such as making photocopies, collecting materials, or scheduling guest speakers and field trips. | ☐ Develop a process for coming to consensus on important issues.
☐ Create a SMART goal that identifies a problem of practice that the team will study together and details a clear plan for working through a cycle of inquiry around that problem of practice.
☐ Decide on a small set of core team practices—instructional strategies that will be used in all classrooms regardless of teacher. | • "Tool: Fist-to-Five Rating Scale" (page 29)
• "Tool: Building Consensus Around Difficult Decisions" (pages 38–39)
• "Tool: SMART Goal Worksheet" (page 69)
• "Tool: Developing a Tiered Lesson Plan" (pages 207–209) |
| Developing Common Assessments | ☐ Teams ask, "What does mastery of our essential outcomes look like in action?"
☐ Conflict can arise around the characteristics of quality instruction and the importance of individual objectives.
☐ Teachers can disagree about the best way to teach and assess individual concepts. | ☐ Develop a short common assessment together that is tied to specific essential outcomes and details common misconceptions that students are likely to have when working with those outcomes.
☐ Identify a tool that can be used to turn teacher observations into actionable data.
☐ Develop sets of proficiency scales and exemplars that serve as tangible expressions of a team's shared definitions of mastery for each essential outcome.
☐ Select a tool for working through conflict with one another. | • "Tool: Resolving Conflict With a Colleague" (page 40)
• "Tool: Developing Exemplars to Standardize Expectations" (page 64)
• "Tool: Building a Common Formative Assessment" (page 102)
• "Tool: Performance Tracking Table" (page 105)
• "Tool: Using Proficiency Scales to Define Levels of Mastery" (page 198) |

Stage of Team Development	Characteristics of This Stage	Next Steps Worth Taking	Resources Worth Exploring
Analyzing Student Learning	☐ Teams ask, "Are students learning what they are supposed to be learning?" ☐ Teams shift attention from a focus on teaching to a focus on learning. ☐ Teachers examine student learning results with one another. ☐ Teachers can be defensive in the face of evidence that students aren't mastering essential outcomes. ☐ Teachers can grow competitive over learning results.	☐ Identify tools and protocols that can be used to structure all data conversations. ☐ Reach out to other school professionals—principals, instructional coaches, curriculum coordinators—for help with spotting trends in student learning data. ☐ Encourage teachers to use student learning data to identify strengths and weaknesses in their pedagogical practices.	• "Tool: Spotting Patterns in Standardized Tests and Universal Screening Data" (pages 83–84) • "Tool: Common Formative Assessment Data Tracker—Individual Results" (pages 109–111) • "Tool: Common Formative Assessment Data Tracker—Team Results" (pages 112–113) • "Tool: Team Analysis of Common Formative Assessment Data" (pages 116–117) • "Tool: Individual Teacher Reflection on Student Learning Data" (page 123)
Differentiating Follow-Up	☐ Teams ask, "What can we do to help more students learn our essential outcomes?" ☐ Teams take collective action rather than responding to results as individuals. ☐ Teams work through cycles of collective inquiry, identifying essential standards, developing strategies to assess progress toward mastering those standards, and providing students with intervention or extension opportunities for each essential outcome.	☐ Develop clear lists of prerequisites and extensions for every essential outcome that you have identified together. ☐ Generate lists of concepts that students are struggling with in each of the units that team members teach. ☐ Develop and evaluate instructional strategies used to provide students with intervention or extension. ☐ Regroup students across your team for intervention and extension experiences. ☐ Incorporate student self-assessment into classroom practices.	• "Tool: Prerequisites and Extensions for an Essential Outcome" (page 157) • "Tool: Tier 2 Intervention Tracking by Individual Teacher" (pages 158–161) • "Tool: List of Common Misconceptions for an Essential Outcome" (page 163) • "Tool: Rating the Effectiveness of Interventions on Your Learning Team" (page 164) • "Tool: Using Where Am I Going? Checklists to Differentiate Learning Experiences" (page 180) • "Tool: Assessment Analysis Form" (page 182)

The Big Book of Tools for Collaborative Teams in a PLC at Work © 2020 Solution Tree Press • SolutionTree.com
Visit **go.SolutionTree.com/PLCbooks/BBTCT** and enter the unique access code found on the book's inside front cover to access this reproducible.

| Reflecting on Instruction | ☐ Teams ask, "What instructional practices work best with our students?"
 ☐ Learning is connected back to teaching.
 ☐ Practitioners engage in deep reflection about instruction.
 ☐ Action research and lesson study are used to document the most effective instructional strategies for a school's student population. | ☐ Use data to identify instructional practices that are having a positive impact on the students you serve.
 ☐ Use data to identify instructional practices that should be abandoned because they are not having a positive impact on the students you serve.
 ☐ Observe one another teaching the same lesson.
 ☐ Publicize the findings of your team's studies to spread knowledge of high-quality instruction across your faculty. | • "Tool: Instructional Implications of Common Formative Assessment Data" (pages 121–122)
 • "Tool: Evidence of Practice in Action" (pages 138–139)
 • "Tool: Evidence of Practice in Action— Teacher Self-Reflection" (pages 140–141)
 • "Tool: Practice-Centered Peer Observation" (pages 142–143) |

Reference

Graham, P., & Ferriter, W. M. (2008). One step at a time: Many professional learning teams pass through these seven stages. *Journal of Staff Development, 29*(3), 38–42.

Strengthening the Collegial Practices of Learning Teams

Odds are that over the last five years, your school or district has rolled out dozens of different change efforts. You might have been introduced to different ways to integrate technology into your instruction or to incorporate complex text into every lesson. Your school has probably embraced some version of project-based learning or personalized learning or blended learning or brain-based learning or game-based learning. My guess is that you have been exposed to genius hours and makerspaces and design thinking, studied growth mindsets and flexible seating and student-centered learning, and rethought your grading practices, your discipline policies, and your strategies for communicating with parents.

That's the pattern in education, isn't it? Driven to create spaces where *all* students can learn at higher levels regardless of their backgrounds or abilities, we chase every new initiative. Some of those practices take root and become a fundamental part of the work that we do with students. But many are replaced almost as quickly as they are adopted. The key to improvement, then, rests in our ability to identify change efforts that really *are* worth investing in.

For Roland S. Barth (2006), founder of the Harvard Graduate School of Education and the Harvard Principals' Center, the most important investment that we can make isn't into new projects or programs at all. Instead, the most important investment that we can make is in the relationships that we have with our colleagues: "The nature of the relationships among the adults within a school has a greater influence on the character and quality of the school and on student accomplishment than anything else" (Barth, 2006, p. 8). Those relationships, Barth (2006) argues, typically fall into one of four categories.

1. **Parallel play:** Parallel play is a concept Barth borrowed from literature on the development of preschool students. Two toddlers sitting next to each other in the same sandbox but playing independently are engaging in parallel play. Sure, they are engaged in the same task—but they aren't working together. In fact, at times they don't even seem to be aware that they are sharing the same space with someone else. As strange as borrowing a concept from preschool development may seem, parallel play probably sounds familiar to you. It is the two teachers who work across the hall from each other for eight hours a day, year after year, without ever showing any real interest in what is happening in each other's classrooms.

2. **Adversarial relationships:** Some adversarial relationships between teachers are self-explanatory and easy to spot. It is the two teachers who openly criticize each other in front of parents, principals, or peers. But others are subtler, characterized by the withholding of resources or information. It is the veteran teachers who refuse to share lesson plans with the struggling rookies next door or the teachers who discover a highly effective teaching practice and then keep the strategy to themselves.

3. **Congenial relationships:** Congenial relationships are the most common relationships in many schools. It is the team of teachers who gather on Friday afternoons at the local coffee shop to celebrate the end of the week or who bring in homemade cookies to celebrate special occasions with one another. It is the colleagues who are willing to drop everything to prepare emergency substitute plans for peers who are out unexpectedly. It is the school where all staff members wear their faculty T-shirts and cheer with pride at the annual districtwide kickoff to the new year. While there is nothing fundamentally wrong with congenial relationships—in fact, pleasant experiences with agreeable people can help us look forward to our workday—they have little impact on improving practice.

4. **Collegial relationships:** Collegial relationships are those that really do improve classroom practice. It is the teacher who finds peers and commits to studying instruction with them. It is the team that spends time researching and testing and revising teaching strategies together. It is the group of colleagues who willingly share knowledge of their craft with one another—and who are genuinely interested in seeing one another succeed. For collegial teachers, relationships are more than personal. They are powerful tools for building pedagogical capacity.

If a collaborative team in a PLC at Work wants to develop a strong sense of collective teacher efficacy, members must minimize parallel play and adversarial relationships while strengthening collegial behaviors. So, what does *strengthening collegial behaviors* look like in action? It is the team that has a clear set of norms that members agree to that defines their expectations for one another. It is the team that develops a specific process for resolving conflict. It is the team that keeps its meetings focused and chooses agenda items deliberately. Collaborative teams leave nothing about strengthening collegial behaviors to chance. Instead, they put explicit structures in place to manage personalities, create consensus, and develop a positive team identity. Two of the most important structures for teams to put into place are a set of team norms and a process for building consensus around difficult decisions.

Developing Team Norms

Norms are the common patterns of participation that define the shared work of any group. Sometimes, those patterns are positive, encouraging collective inquiry around practice. Other times, those patterns are negative, preventing teachers from learning from one another. Developing a clear set of norms is essential for ensuring that a group functions in a way that meets the individual needs and expectations of each of its members. When teams fail to develop clear norms, members can feel frustrated about collaborating with others.

For learning community expert Daniel R. Venables (2011), developing norms can be done in two steps.

1. **Sharing pet peeves and essential traits:** Venables (2011) recommends that teams begin their norm-setting process by allowing members to share both the kinds of behaviors that drive them crazy while working in groups and the key traits that others will notice about them while working in groups. Sharing our peeves and traits, as he calls them, early in a norm-setting process can help make individual needs and expectations transparent to everyone on the team.

2. **Brainstorming four to six norms:** After identifying the peeves and traits of individual members, Venables (2011) recommends that teams brainstorm a list of four to six expectations that will govern the shared work of a learning team. Limiting a list of norms to fewer than six expectations forces teams to prioritize the behaviors that they hope to see out of one another, and it makes it easier for individuals to adhere to the expectations of their colleagues. Longer lists of norms quickly become irrelevant or ignored because they are impossible to remember.

See page 21 for a tool to help your team develop its own set of norms.

Building Consensus Around Difficult Decisions

Achieving consensus on difficult decisions that affect the entire team is one of the most challenging aspects of collaborating around practice. To build consensus, collaborative teams engage in deliberate conversations designed to ensure that the opinions, ideas, and concerns of every team member are heard, valued, and addressed.

Those conversations generally depend on these three core behaviors.

1. **Establishing clarity:** Building consensus around an important decision starts by developing a shared sense of the decision that your team is trying to make.

2. **Identifying non-negotiables:** Building consensus around an important decision also depends on recognizing any non-negotiables that members of your team have before your conversation even begins. By allowing all team members to state what matters most to them about the decision that you are making, you are more likely to brainstorm potential solutions that take into account the individual needs of your peers, and to avoid potential solutions that have little to no chance of being embraced by everyone on your team.

3. **Listing areas of agreement:** Finally, building consensus around an important decision depends on finding common ground. Listing the areas where your team already agrees can give you a valuable starting point for developing solutions that everyone can embrace.

Once teams have established clarity, identified non-negotiables, and listed areas of agreement, they can develop informed solutions that all members of their team are likely to embrace. See page 38 for a tool to help guide your team through this process.

Resources for Strengthening the Collegial Practices of Learning Teams

The resources in this chapter are all designed to strengthen the general collegial behaviors on learning teams. The five fundamentals for strengthening the collegial practices of your team include the following.

1. **"Tool: Developing Team Norms"** (pages 21–23)—One of the most important steps that collaborative teams take is to explicitly state how team members will act in common collaborative situations. Use this template created using the work of Venables (2011) to develop positive norms for your learning team.

2. **"Tool: Establishing Team Roles"** (pages 24–26)—Collaborative teams are defined by their ability to generate and test new ideas with one another.

Generating and testing new ideas efficiently and effectively depends on having a clearly defined set of roles that individual members fill for one another. Use this template to identify individuals on your learning team who are uniquely suited to fill each of those roles.

3. **"Tool: Learning Team Meeting Notes"** (pages 27–28)—One simple tool that all learning teams should use is an agenda for recording notes during their regularly scheduled meetings. Detailed meeting notes provide a long-term record of team actions and decisions that can be referred to over time to document progress and to identify next steps worth taking. Use this template to record notes during your next meeting.

4. **"Tool: Fist-to-Five Rating Scale"** (page 29)—Collaborative teams are constantly making shared decisions. In order to facilitate this decision making, they also develop a quick strategy for allowing members to express individual levels of agreement—or the lack thereof—with the direction that the team is heading in. This rating scale can fill that role on your learning team (Graham & Ferriter, 2010).

5. **"Checklist: Tasks Teams Can Tackle During Collaborative Meetings"** (pages 30–31)—Explicitly structuring collaboration to improve classroom practice depends on tying every agenda item during weekly meetings to the four critical questions of learning in a PLC at Work. Use this checklist to identify specific tasks tied to each critical question that your team is ready to tackle.

The following are additional resources for strengthening the collegial practices of your team.

- **"Tool: Team Task Tracking"** (page 33)—Over time, studying practice together can feel static to members of learning teams. To avoid professional stagnation, use this template to keep track of the kinds of tasks that you are engaging in during your regular meetings and to identify new practices worth integrating into your work.

- **"Tool: Team Meeting Evaluation Strips"** (page 34)—Collaborative teams regularly monitor the quality of their meetings. Without regular monitoring, it is impossible to keep moving in a productive direction. Consider asking each team member to fill out one of these evaluation strips at the end of every meeting. Turn in the strips to your team leader, who can then lead future conversations about the data collected.

- **"Checklist: Professional Development for Learning Teams"** (pages 35–36)—The work of learning teams presents new challenges that must be addressed with systematic professional development. Team members must acquire two broad categories of skills: (1) team-based collaboration skills and (2) skills for instructional reflection. Use this checklist to indicate the kinds of professional development that you believe would best move your team forward.

- **"Tool: Record of Team Accomplishments"** (page 37)—One truth that often gets overlooked in PLCs is that the persistent work of collaborative teams is challenging. The result: teams that don't find regular opportunities for celebration often end up frustrated with one another and with the process. To help your team avoid this collaborative trap, use this template to keep a running record of your shared successes.

- **"Tool: Building Consensus Around Difficult Decisions"** (pages 38–39)— Moving forward on difficult decisions depends on teams that are skilled at establishing clarity, identifying non-negotiables, and listing areas of agreement. Use this template the next time your learning team is struggling to make a difficult decision together.

- **"Tool: Resolving Conflict With a Colleague"** (page 40)—Conflict is an unavoidable by-product of collaboration between professionals who are passionate about their work. Inevitably, there will be moments where disagreements happen on every learning team. The good news is that resolving conflict productively strengthens your relationships with others. Use this template to plan a conversation designed to resolve a conflict that you are currently having with a colleague.

- **"Tool: What Is Your Team Monitoring?"** (pages 41–43)—Collaborative learning teams are deliberate about focusing their time and attention on the work that matters most. To help your team remain focused on the right work, use this template to reflect on the value of every program, initiative, action, school requirement, or team decision that is consuming your time and attention.

- **"Tool: Learning Team Quarterly Reflection"** (page 44)—Leadership expert Dan Rockwell (2017) argues that groups interested in driving positive change should regularly answer four simple questions together: (1) What should we keep doing? (2) What do we need to improve? (3) What do we need to stop doing? and (4) What do we need to start doing? To strengthen the work of your learning team, use this template to answer those questions once each quarter.

- **"Survey: The State of Your Learning Team"** (pages 45–47)—Strengthening the collegial behaviors of a learning team depends on carefully monitoring the work that you are doing with one another. Use this survey to collect information on the progress that your learning team is making together, and then use the information that you gather to plan a customized next step for yourselves.

- **"Survey: The Trust on Your Learning Team"** (page 48)—Trust among members is essential for moving from parallel play and adversarial relationships to strong collegial teams committed to studying practice together. Use this survey to get a sense of the levels of trust on your learning team.

Five Fundamental Resources

for Strengthening the Collegial

Practices of Learning Teams

Tool: Developing Team Norms

Step 1: Sharing Your Pet Peeves and Essential Traits

Instructions: In a team meeting, all members should share one pet peeve that they have while working in groups with others and one essential trait that others will notice while working in a group with them. Those peeves and traits should be recorded in the following chart by your team's notetaker. They will be used to develop norms in step 2.

Team Member	Pet Peeve	Essential Trait
Sample: Bill Ferriter	*Sample:* It drives me nuts when people are on their devices while we are engaged in important conversations.	*Sample:* I make decisions quickly and am almost always ready to move on. That can drive people who need more think time than me crazy.

Five Fundamental Resources
Strengthening the Collegial Practices of Learning Teams

Questions for Team Reflection

Do you notice any patterns in the behavior of other team members that are pet peeves for you? What are they and why do you think they bother you?

What patterns in your own behavior are likely to bother other members of your learning team? Why?

What are some common actions you will need to take to make sure that your meetings feel productive to all team members?

Step 2: Brainstorming Your Norms

Instructions: Now, brainstorm four to six norms that describe how your team will respond when working through common team processes. Remember that norms are explicit statements designed to address the peeves and traits that your team detailed in step 1. If followed, your norms should create a working environment that honors and respects the needs of the individual members of your learning team.

Common Team Behaviors and Processes Brainstorm a norm for each of the following common team behaviors and processes.	Sample Norm	Our Norm
Making Shared Decisions	We will use our fist-to-five rating scale to give everyone the opportunity to express their level of agreement with shared decisions.	

Five Fundamental Resources
Strengthening the Collegial Practices of Learning Teams

Handling Disagreements	We won't move forward with important decisions until everyone has had the chance to be heard and to offer alternatives to the ideas. we are considering.	
Showing Respect to One Another	We will be active contributors in every meeting, adding thoughts, offering suggestions, and sharing our opinions.	
Structuring Our Meetings	We will have a clear agenda for every meeting, with no more than three items.	
Other: Use this space to create a norm for other common behaviors or processes that your team addresses on a regular basis.		

Questions for Reflection

Which of your team's norms will be the easiest for you to follow? Which will be hardest?

Based on your team's unique set of peeves and traits, which of your norms will be the most important to ensure that your collaborative work feels productive for everyone?

How will you hold each other accountable for adhering to your team's norms? How will you celebrate moments when members are following your team's norms?

Source: Adapted from Venables, D. R. (2011). The practice of authentic PLCs: A guide to effective teacher teams. Thousand Oaks, CA: Corwin Press.

Five Fundamental Resources

Strengthening the Collegial Practices of Learning Teams

Tool: Establishing Team Roles

Instructions: Listed in the following template are five roles—(1) team leader, (2) challenger, (3) producer, (4) encourager, and (5) realist—that all collaborative teams need if they are going to be productive. Working together, record all members of your team who have the skills and dispositions to fill each role. That way, you can maximize your collaborative potential by ensuring that all members are doing work that matches both their personalities and their professional abilities. Remember that on small teams, some members may need to fill more than one role.

Name of Role	Description of Role	Skills Necessary for Filling Role	Members Suited for Filling Role
Team Leader	• Organizes agendas for weekly meetings • Addresses conflict between team members • Leads consensus-building conversations • Keeps the team focused on yearly goals	☐ Strong relationship builder ☐ Good sense of the overall direction of both the team and the school ☐ Willingness to listen to all perspectives ☐ Commitment to seeing everyone move forward together	
Team Challenger	• Challenges the current practices of the learning team • Contributes to or leads brainstorming of new alternatives and approaches worth considering • Regularly asks, "What if we tried _____?" when the team is working to generate new ideas	☐ Strong professional knowledge base and learning network to draw ideas from ☐ Good sense of the professional strengths and weaknesses of the learning team ☐ Ability to look at data summarizing the team's current reality and offer logical suggestions for next steps	

The Big Book of Tools for Collaborative Teams in a PLC at Work © 2020 Solution Tree Press • SolutionTree.com

Visit **go.SolutionTree.com/PLCbooks** to download this free reproducible.

Five Fundamental Resources
Strengthening the Collegial Practices of Learning Teams

Team Producer	• Takes notes during meetings • Develops a logical system for organizing the team's shared documents • Produces first drafts of shared documents for the team's review • Finds ways to accurately communicate team decisions	☐ Skilled with all kinds of document creation: Google Docs, PowerPoints, PDFs, and so on ☐ Logical thinker with strong organizational skills ☐ Good at listening to and summarizing ideas generated in group conversations ☐ Able to participate in conversations and create content at the same time	
Team Encourager	• Provides words of encouragement and affirmation both during and beyond weekly meetings • Moves the team forward during moments of stagnation or apathy • Monitors the attitudes and workloads of individual members and provides support when necessary	☐ Generally optimistic; skilled at finding things worth celebrating regardless of the circumstance ☐ Strong relationships with—and genuine concern for—all members of the team ☐ Willingness to always find time to lend a hand when others need help	
Team Realist	• Evaluates team decisions against the current workload of the team • Questions team decisions that seem unrealistic or impossible to pull off • Gives voice to concerns that might otherwise go unspoken	☐ Ability to understand the work capacity of the learning team ☐ Strong sense of all the different projects and initiatives that the team is currently tackling ☐ Ability to express skepticism, concern, and doubt in a professional way	

The Big Book of Tools for Collaborative Teams in a PLC at Work © 2020 Solution Tree Press • SolutionTree.com
Visit **go.SolutionTree.com/PLCbooks** to download this free reproducible.

Questions for Reflection

Are there any roles that your team will have no trouble filling? How will that help your team?

Are there any roles that will be difficult for your team to fill? How might that hurt your team?

Do you think that rotating team roles is important? Why or why not? How would rotating team roles help your team? How would rotating roles hurt your team?

Are there any roles that aren't listed here that you think your team will need in order to be successful? What are they? Why are those roles important for your team?

page 1 of 2

Tool: Learning Team Meeting Notes

Instructions: High-functioning teams use notes taken by their team's producer during weekly meetings to focus their time together, to document their shared decisions, and to create a set of action steps for moving their work forward. Use the following template to create a regular record of your team's meetings.

Learning Team:	Our Team Norms:
Date:	
Members Present:	
Members Absent:	

Agenda Item 1	Team Discussion, Conclusions, and Agreements	Actions to Be Taken
Which core collaborative behavior does this agenda item address? (Check one.) ☐ General team tasks ☐ Defining essential learning outcomes ☐ Developing common formative assessments ☐ Discussing instructional strategies ☐ Looking at student work ☐ Reviewing and responding to data ☐ Planning remediation or extension tasks ☐ Other:		

Five Fundamental Resources
Strengthening the Collegial Practices of Learning Teams

Five Fundamental Resources
Strengthening the Collegial Practices of Learning Teams

page 2 of 2

Agenda Item 2	Team Discussion, Conclusions, and Agreements	Actions to Be Taken
Which core collaborative behavior does this agenda item address? (Check one.) ☐ General team tasks ☐ Defining essential learning outcomes ☐ Developing common formative assessments ☐ Discussing instructional strategies ☐ Looking at student work ☐ Reviewing and responding to data ☐ Planning remediation or extension tasks ☐ Other:		

Agenda Item 3	Team Discussion, Conclusions, and Agreements	Actions to Be Taken
Which core collaborative behavior does this agenda item address? (Check one.) ☐ General team tasks ☐ Defining essential learning outcomes ☐ Developing common formative assessments ☐ Discussing instructional strategies ☐ Looking at student work ☐ Reviewing and responding to data ☐ Planning remediation or extension tasks ☐ Other:		

Five Fundamental Resources
Strengthening the Collegial Practices of Learning Teams

Tool: Fist-to-Five Rating Scale

Instructions: Each time your team makes important decisions, ask members to rate their level of agreement with your team's direction on a scale from 0 (make a fist) to 5 (hold up all five fingers). Use the following descriptors to decide on the rating that you will give to your important decisions.

Rating	Descriptor
5	**Why didn't we make this decision sooner?** This decision is great, and we've got the capacity to make it happen without investing a ton of new effort. I've fallen in love with this decision and I'm willing to lead any efforts to make it become reality.
4	**This is a decision that I completely support:** I really believe that this decision aligns well with our school's mission and just know it is going to help our students succeed. I'm willing to move forward and am also willing to put some time, energy, and effort into helping make this happen.
3	**I believe in this decision but question our timing:** I think this is a great decision worth pursuing—I'm just not sure that this is the right time to move forward. I'm excited to see where this decision goes, but I think we should set it aside for now. I won't be opposed if others invest energy into making this happen, but I can't promise that I'll help.
2	**I'm not totally comfortable with this decision, but I can see it has merit:** I'm willing to move forward with the decision as it currently stands, and I won't put any barriers in our team's way as we work to make this happen, but I'm probably going to need some practical and philosophical support before I'll completely embrace this action.
1	**This is a decision that I have strong reservations about:** While I can see some potential in taking this action, there are several things that we need to consider before I can be comfortable with this. Can we do a bit more talking before moving forward, please?
0	**There is no way I could possibly support this decision:** In fact, I think that supporting this decision would be irresponsible because it doesn't align with our school's mission and may even harm our students. We shouldn't even consider this action if needed.

Note to teams: If any member rates a decision a 3 or less, *you haven't reached a consensus yet*. When that happens, you must continue your conversations with one another. Members with concerns should be ready to articulate them to the team. The remaining members should be ready to take those concerns into account and to make changes to your team's decision if needed.

Questions for Reflection

Are there members of your team who feel hesitant about this decision? How do you know? What will you do to elicit their thinking and to honor their positions?

What changes would you be willing to make to your own position around this issue? Remember that flexibility is a key trait to building consensus.

Source: Adapted from Graham, P., & Ferriter, W. M. (2010). Building a Professional Learning Community at Work: A guide to the first year. *Bloomington, IN: Solution Tree Press.*

Checklist: Tasks Teams Can Tackle During Collaborative Meetings

Instructions: Reflect on the work that your learning team is doing by placing a *checkmark* next to tasks you are already tackling and a *star* next to tasks that you are ready to tackle. *Cross out* tasks that are currently beyond the collaborative ability of your learning team. Then use the reflection questions to help your team identify next steps worth taking.

Five Fundamental Resources
Strengthening the Collegial Practices of Learning Teams

Critical Question 1: What do we want our students to learn during this upcoming unit (DuFour, DuFour, Eaker, Many, & Mattos, 2016)?	Critical Question 2: How will we know that our students are learning during this upcoming unit (DuFour et al., 2016)?
Potential collaborative tasks:	Potential collaborative tasks:
☐ Work through curriculum materials to identify outcomes that are essential for students to learn.	☐ Develop unit pretests that can be used to identify levels of mastery before we even begin teaching.
☐ Work through curriculum materials to identify outcomes that are "nice to knows," but that don't deserve priority attention.	☐ Develop short (four- to five-question) common formative assessments for every essential outcome.
☐ Rewrite essential outcomes in language that everyone—teachers, parents, students, peers working in other grade levels—can understand.	☐ Develop rubrics or proficiency scales that define different levels of performance on each essential outcome.
☐ Develop teacher pacing guidelines that include tentative starting dates, ending dates, and dates for common assessments for each unit.	☐ Develop exemplars of subjective tasks representing different levels of performance to standardize our grading.
☐ Use the team's expertise to identify critical skills and work behaviors that students must master in order to be successful learners.	☐ Develop a system for recording observations of student performance to use as evidence of mastery.
☐ Develop a system for sharing two or three promising instructional strategies for each objective, skill, or work behavior we identify as essential.	☐ Experiment with digital tools for assessing and reporting on student learning.
	☐ Develop a system for organizing, reflecting on, and acting around common formative assessment data.
Critical Question 3: How will we respond when students struggle during this upcoming unit (DuFour et al., 2016)?	**Critical Question 4: How will we respond when students excel during this upcoming unit (DuFour et al., 2016)?**
Potential collaborative tasks:	Potential collaborative tasks:
☐ Maintain lists of students who have yet to master each essential outcome in a unit of study.	☐ Maintain lists of students who demonstrate mastery of essential outcomes on unit pretests.
☐ Maintain lists of common misconceptions or mistakes for each essential outcome.	☐ Maintain lists of additional concepts that can extend student thinking for each essential outcome.
☐ Share one promising instructional strategy for reteaching essential outcomes.	☐ Share one promising instructional strategy for providing extension of essential outcomes.

- ☐ Identify one instructional strategy for teaching concepts that was ineffective.
- ☐ Develop additional assessments to measure progress after interventions have been delivered.
- ☐ Experiment with digital tools for delivering short remedial lessons to struggling students.

- ☐ Develop sets of challenge tasks for each essential outcome that students who are working beyond the required curriculum can complete independently.
- ☐ Develop additional assessments to measure progress after extensions have been delivered.
- ☐ Experiment with digital tools for delivering short extension lessons to excelling students.

Questions for Reflection

Review your learning team's recent meeting agendas. Make a list of the kinds of tasks that you are currently working on with one another.

How often is your learning team tackling one of the tasks included on this tool? What is preventing your learning team from tackling tasks included on this tool more frequently?

What tasks on this tool is your learning team ready to tackle? Why are those the right tasks for your learning team to engage with right now?

What tasks on this tool rest beyond the current ability of your learning team? Why are these tasks too difficult for your learning team to tackle right now?

Reference

DuFour, R., DuFour, R., Eaker, R., Many, T. W., & Mattos, M. (2016). *Learning by doing: A handbook for Professional Learning Communities at Work* (3rd ed.). Bloomington, IN: Solution Tree Press.

Additional Resources

for Strengthening the Collegial

Practices of Learning Teams

Tool: Team Task Tracking

Instructions: The best way to ensure that your collaborative work doesn't become stagnant is to look for patterns in the kinds of tasks that you are completing with one another during your regular meetings. Over the next quarter, record the date in the appropriate row every time that you tackle one of these tasks in a team meeting. Then, during your next quarterly reflection, use the data that you collect and the reflection questions at the bottom of this template to determine next steps worth taking together.

When was the last time that your learning team . . .						
Revisited or revised your norms together?						
Read or reflected on a professional article together?						
Defined essential learning outcomes for an upcoming unit of study together?						
Wrote a common assessment together?						
Used a protocol to look at common assessment results or student work samples together?						
Planned a remediation or extension activity together?						
Developed a set of exemplars or proficiency scales for subjective tasks together?						
Took time to intentionally celebrate your successes?						

Questions for Reflection

Where is your team spending the bulk of its collaborative time? Are you spending more time on some tasks than others? Are there any tasks that your team hasn't tackled yet? What tasks would you like to see your team take on moving forward?

The Big Book of Tools for Collaborative Teams in a PLC at Work © 2020 Solution Tree Press • SolutionTree.com
Visit **go.SolutionTree.com/PLCbooks/BBTCT** and enter the unique access code found on the book's inside front cover to access this reproducible.

Additional Resources — Strengthening the Collegial Practices of Learning Teams

Tool: Team Meeting Evaluation Strips

Instructions: After making as many copies as you need, cut out each evaluation strip, and distribute the strips to your team members at the end of each meeting. Once members have completed their evaluation strips, they can return them to the team leader, who will use the data collected to plan for and lead future conversations about the quality of your work together.

Meeting Evaluation and Planning				
We stuck to our agenda.	Yes	No	What did we do particularly well during today's meeting?	What can we do to improve our next meeting?
Everyone participated.	Yes	No		
We completed important tasks.	Yes	No		
We set a plan for our next meeting.	Yes	No		
This meeting was productive.	Yes	No		
Meeting Evaluation and Planning				
We stuck to our agenda.	Yes	No	What did we do particularly well during today's meeting?	What can we do to improve our next meeting?
Everyone participated.	Yes	No		
We completed important tasks.	Yes	No		
We set a plan for our next meeting.	Yes	No		
This meeting was productive.	Yes	No		
Meeting Evaluation and Planning				
We stuck to our agenda.	Yes	No	What did we do particularly well during today's meeting?	What can we do to improve our next meeting?
Everyone participated.	Yes	No		
We completed important tasks.	Yes	No		
We set a plan for our next meeting.	Yes	No		
This meeting was productive.	Yes	No		

Additional Resources
Strengthening the Collegial Practices of Learning Teams

Checklist: Professional Development for Learning Teams

Instructions: Working individually, identify your team's professional development needs by selecting one to three items from each of the following lists. Then, use the reflection questions at the end of this template as a guide for a team conversation about professional development priorities.

Team Name: _____	Teacher Name (optional): _____
My team needs immediate support in . . .	

Team-Based Collaboration Skills

- ☐ Developing team norms and protocols
- ☐ Determining how group conversations and meetings are structured
- ☐ Determining how violations of team norms are addressed
- ☐ Determining how the results of the team's work are recorded
- ☐ Conducting effective conversations
- ☐ Finding common ground and working toward consensus
- ☐ Depersonalizing discussions of curricular, assessment, and instructional practices
- ☐ Finding ways to celebrate and sustain the efforts of our learning team
- ☐ Building trust between colleagues
- ☐ Setting goals and reflecting on results
- ☐ Uncovering hidden disagreements
- ☐ Embracing conflict as an opportunity for continued growth
- ☐ Using protocols to set priorities
- ☐ Conducting team-based, self-directed action research or lesson study
- ☐ Amplifying "lessons learned" across our entire grade level or department
- ☐ Understanding the characteristics of adult learners and continuing education
- ☐ Other:

Skills for Instructional Reflection

- ☐ Identifying required state and district curricular expectations
- ☐ Prioritizing learning objectives based on an understanding of our students
- ☐ Designing a logical sequence for addressing required elements of the curriculum
- ☐ Understanding the difference between formative and summative assessment
- ☐ Connecting assessments to specific learning goals
- ☐ Measuring higher-order-thinking skills
- ☐ Developing performance-based assessments
- ☐ Using data collection and analysis tools to track progress by student and by standard
- ☐ Developing discussion protocols for conversations related to data
- ☐ Identifying common areas of student mastery and misunderstanding
- ☐ Understanding the unique characteristics of both low and high achievers
- ☐ Defining strategies and identifying tools for differentiating lesson plans
- ☐ Investigating the relationships between instructional practices and student learning outcomes
- ☐ Developing protocols for lesson study, action research, and peer observations
- ☐ Other:

Additional Resources Strengthening the Collegial Practices of Learning Teams

page 1 of 2

The Big Book of Tools for Collaborative Teams in a PLC at Work © 2020 Solution Tree Press • SolutionTree.com
Visit **go.SolutionTree.com/PLCbooks/BBTCT** and enter the unique access code found on the book's inside front cover to access this reproducible.

Questions for Reflection

What patterns can you spot in the professional development needs identified by the individual members of your learning team? Are there individual skills that were identified as a need by multiple members of your team? What were they?

Does your team need more support with team-based collaboration skills or with skills for instructional reflection? Why?

What steps can you take to get the support that you need in order to improve your collaborative skill set? Who will you reach out to for help? When will you act?

Source: Adapted from Graham, P., & Ferriter, W. M. (2010). Building a Professional Learning Community at Work: A guide to the first year. *Bloomington, IN: Solution Tree Press.*

page 2 of 2

The Big Book of Tools for Collaborative Teams in a PLC at Work © 2020 Solution Tree Press • SolutionTree.com
Visit **go.SolutionTree.com/PLCbooks/BBTCT** and enter the unique access code found on the book's inside front cover to access this reproducible.

Additional Resources
Strengthening the Collegial Practices of Learning Teams

Tool: Record of Team Accomplishments

Instructions: In the left column, enter one of your team's accomplishments for each row. In the column titled **Impact**, record how this accomplishment positively affected your students, colleagues, or school. Next, in the column titled **Recognition**, acknowledge those team members who deserve extra recognition for their work on this accomplishment. Finally, under **Next Steps**, think about and write down ideas on how your team can build on this accomplishment, and what steps you can take to move your work forward.

Our Accomplishment	Impact	Recognition	Next Steps
Sample: We finished identifying essential standards for an upcoming unit of study.	*Sample:* Now that we have a clear set of essential standards, we will be able to focus our work on helping all students master important outcomes.	*Sample:* We are grateful for Javon, who did a great job coming up with a format for the document that we are using to list our essential outcomes.	*Sample:* Our next step is to keep developing sets of essential outcomes for all the units in our required curriculum.

Additional Resources Strengthening the Collegial Practices of Learning Teams

The Big Book of Tools for Collaborative Teams in a PLC at Work © 2020 Solution Tree Press • SolutionTree.com

Visit **go.SolutionTree.com/PLCbooks/BBTCT** and enter the unique access code found on the book's inside front cover to access this reproducible.

Tool: Building Consensus Around Difficult Decisions

Step 1: Establish Clarity

Instructions: Work together to write a clear statement of the decision that you are making.

Step 2: Identify Non-Negotiables

Instructions: Ask all team members to describe the factors that matter the most to them about the decision that you are making. What characteristics would a potential solution require to earn their support?

Team Member	What Matters Most About the Decision We Are Making?

The Big Book of Tools for Collaborative Teams in a PLC at Work © 2020 Solution Tree Press • SolutionTree.com
Visit **go.SolutionTree.com/PLCbooks/BBTCT** and enter the unique access code found on the book's inside front cover to access this reproducible.

Step 3: List Areas of Agreement

Instructions: Work together to find the common ground that already exists among the various thoughts and opinions of your team members. The non-negotiables generated in step 2 will help you identify where your team members agree.

We already agree on the following core ideas related to the decision that we are trying to make:

Step 4: Develop Two Proposed Solutions

Instructions: Develop two proposed solutions for the decision that you are trying to make that take the non-negotiables of your team members and your areas of agreement into account.

Proposed Solution 1		Proposed Solution 2
	or	

Step 5: Summarize Your Final Decision

Instructions: After discussing the two potential solutions brainstormed in step 4, summarize your final decision in the following box.

Here is what we have agreed to do:

Tool: Resolving Conflict With a Colleague

Instructions: Once you are finished thinking through the following questions, initiate a dialogue with a colleague who you disagree with. Use your answers to these questions to guide a solutions-focused conversation with the colleague.

Questions	Your Response
What do you admire the most about the colleague who you are having a conflict with? What strengths does the colleague bring to your learning team? To the classroom? Resolving a conflict starts by reminding ourselves that our peers are worthy of our respect, not opponents who we need to defeat.	
Describe the issue that is causing conflict between you and your colleague. It is impossible to resolve disagreements until you can accurately explain your own point of view to the colleague who you disagree with.	
Based on your recent interactions, how do you think your colleague would describe the issue that is causing conflict between you? It is also impossible to resolve disagreements until you fully understand the point of view of the colleague who you disagree with.	
What areas of overlap do you think exist between your position and the position of your colleague? Solving conflicts depends on finding areas where you agree with your colleagues, not on pointing out all the places where you disagree with one another.	
What compromise could you and your colleague make that would respect both of your positions? The health of your professional relationship depends on finding a way to move forward together by determining a next step that you are both willing to take.	

The Big Book of Tools for Collaborative Teams in a PLC at Work © 2020 Solution Tree Press • SolutionTree.com

Visit **go.SolutionTree.com/PLCbooks/BBTCT** and enter the unique access code found on the book's inside front cover to access this reproducible.

Additional Resources
Strengthening the Collegial Practices of Learning Teams

Tool: What Is Your Team Monitoring?

Instructions: Beginning in the rows under the column heading **Monitored Initiative**, write down a program, initiative, action, school requirement, or team decision that is occupying your team's time and attention. The column titled **Core Collaborative Behavior That Initiative Addresses** lists tasks that effective learning teams focus time and energy on; use the checkboxes in that column to determine which behaviors the initiative your team is monitoring aligns with. Because collaborative teams must honestly assess the time demands that each initiative places on their collective work, use the checkboxes in the column titled **Time Required to Implement Initiative** to assess the amount of time necessary to make this project work. Finally, keep in mind that collaborative learning teams must make systematic decisions about each project based on its connection to student learning, its alignment with the building's mission and vision, and its compliance with school district mandates. Use the checkboxes at the end of this template to help your team consider each factor and prioritize the initiative. Finally, use the reflection questions at the end of this template to help guide your team in determining next steps.

Monitored Initiative	Core Collaborative Behaviors That Initiative Addresses (Check all that apply.)	Time Required to Implement Initiative	Priority Placed on Initiative
	☐ Identify essential curriculum: deciding what students should learn ☐ Develop common assessments: measuring what students should learn ☐ Monitor student learning data: evaluating what students have learned ☐ Provide remediation or enrichment: ensuring that every student learns ☐ This project doesn't clearly meet any of these goals.	☐ Extensive amounts of time ☐ Moderate amounts of time ☐ Small amounts of time	☐ This task should be at the center of our attention. ☐ This task demands attention, but it isn't a priority. ☐ This task should be set aside for now. ☐ This task should be eliminated or ignored.

page 1 of 3

Additional Resources Strengthening the Collegial Practices of Learning Teams

The Big Book of Tools for Collaborative Teams in a PLC at Work © 2020 Solution Tree Press • SolutionTree.com
Visit **go.SolutionTree.com/PLCbooks/BBTCT** and enter the unique access code found on the book's inside front cover to access this reproducible.

Monitored Initiative	Core Collaborative Behaviors That Initiative Addresses (Check all that apply.)	Time Required to Implement Initiative	Priority Placed on Initiative
	☐ Identify essential curriculum: deciding what students should learn ☐ Develop common assessments: measuring what students should learn ☐ Monitor student learning data: evaluating what students have learned ☐ Provide remediation or enrichment: ensuring that every student learns ☐ This project doesn't clearly meet any of these goals.	☐ Extensive amounts of time ☐ Moderate amounts of time ☐ Small amounts of time	☐ This task should be at the center of our attention. ☐ This task demands attention, but it isn't a priority. ☐ This task should be set aside for now. ☐ This task should be eliminated or ignored.
	☐ Identify essential curriculum: deciding what students should learn ☐ Develop common assessments: measuring what students should learn ☐ Monitor student learning data: evaluating what students have learned ☐ Provide remediation or enrichment: ensuring that every student learns ☐ This project doesn't clearly meet any of these goals.	☐ Extensive amounts of time ☐ Moderate amounts of time ☐ Small amounts of time	☐ This task should be at the center of our attention. ☐ This task demands attention, but it isn't a priority. ☐ This task should be set aside for now. ☐ This task should be eliminated or ignored.

The Big Book of Tools for Collaborative Teams in a PLC at Work © 2020 Solution Tree Press • SolutionTree.com

Visit **go.SolutionTree.com/PLCbooks/BBTCT** and enter the unique access code found on the book's inside front cover to access this reproducible.

page 3 of 3

| | ☐ Identify essential curriculum: deciding what students should learn

☐ Develop common assessments: measuring what students should learn

☐ Monitor student learning data: evaluating what students have learned

☐ Provide remediation or enrichment: ensuring that every student learns

☐ This project doesn't clearly meet any of these goals. | ☐ Extensive amounts of time
☐ Moderate amounts of time
☐ Small amounts of time | ☐ This task should be at the center of our attention.

☐ This task demands attention, but it isn't a priority.

☐ This task should be set aside for now.

☐ This task should be eliminated or ignored. |

Questions for Reflection

Do you notice any patterns in the types of initiatives that your team is currently monitoring? Are you spending most of your time focused on tasks directly related to student learning? Does one type of task dominate your team's attention? Why?

What one task do you wish your team could spend *more* time focused on? How would this help move your learning team forward?

What one task do you wish your team could spend *less* time focused on? What is keeping you from cutting that work from your team's agendas?

Source: Adapted from Graham, P., & Ferriter, W. M. (2010). Building a Professional Learning Community at Work: A guide to the first year. Bloomington, IN: Solution Tree Press.

Additional Resources
Strengthening the Collegial Practices of Learning Teams

Tool: Learning Team Quarterly Reflection

Instructions: As a team, answer the following questions, drawn from the work of leadership expert Dan Rockwell (2017), four times a year.

What do we need to *keep* doing?	What do we need to *improve* on?
Why? What evidence do you have that these efforts are making a difference for teachers? For students?	*Why? What evidence do you have that these efforts could make a difference for teachers and students with a bit of tweaking?*
What should we *stop* doing?	**What should we *start* doing?**
Why? What evidence do you have that these efforts aren't worth the time and energy that we invest in them?	*Why? How would these new actions make a difference for teachers and students? How are they better than the work we have been tackling?*

Additional Resources
Strengthening the Collegial Practices of Learning Teams

Reference

Rockwell, D. (2017, March 16). *How to K.I.S.S. lousy operational meetings goodbye* [Blog post]. Accessed at https://leadershipfreak.blog/2017/03/16/how-to-k-i-s-s-lousy-operational-meetings-goodbye on August 5, 2019.

Survey: The State of Your Learning Team

Instructions: First, please indicate with a checkmark the extent to which you agree with, disagree with, or feel neutral about each indicator in the following survey. Next, please indicate how ready your learning team is to tackle the tasks detailed in each indicator. Finally, answer the reflection questions found at the end of this template. This information will be used to plan customized next steps for each collaborative team in the building.

Name of Learning Team:						
Personal Dynamics	**Disagree**	**Neutral**	**Agree**	**We Aren't Ready for This Yet**	**We Are Ready for This Now**	**We Are Already Doing This**
Our learning team has a well-developed agenda for every meeting that effectively documents our shared decisions.						
Our learning team has a process for gathering honest and open input from all members when making key decisions.						
Our learning team has clearly defined roles for participation in our meetings.						
Our learning team has a process for sharing the workload.						
Our learning team has a process for resolving conflicts.						
Our learning team has a process for giving and receiving critical feedback among team members.						
Our learning team has a common language to use when working through conflict.						
Our learning team has a process for holding team members accountable for making productive contributions.						
Our learning team has a process for determining when we have reached consensus.						
Our learning team has a process for bringing new and challenging ideas into our group.						

Additional Resources Strengthening the Collegial Practices of Learning Teams

Collaborative Task Development	Disagree	Neutral	Agree	We Aren't Ready for This Yet	We Are Ready for This Now	We Are Already Doing This
Our learning team has a SMART (strategic and specific, measurable, attainable, results oriented, and time bound) goal that we set and are working toward together.						
Our learning team has identified essential outcomes for each of the units in the curriculum.						
Our learning team has developed common assessments designed to measure student progress toward mastering our essential outcomes.						
Our learning team has incorporated questions that require higher-level thinking into our common assessments.						
Our learning team uses open-ended assignments for some of our common assessments.						
Our learning team analyzes learning results, looking for trends in both student and teacher performance.						
Our learning team takes action based on the trends that we spot in student learning data.						
Our learning team has developed exemplars that illustrate what student mastery looks like on tasks that are evaluated subjectively.						
Our learning team has practiced grading subjective assignments together to ensure reliability in our scoring.						
Our learning team varies the pacing of our content to support the struggling students and to challenge the most accomplished pupils in our classrooms.						

Questions for Reflection

Please describe your learning team's greatest success to date. What are you the proudest of about the work that you are doing together?

Please describe the stumbling block that is currently holding your learning team back. What could your group be doing better?

Please describe the practices that your learning team is currently the most comfortable with. What has your team already mastered?

What is the most logical next step for your learning team to take? Why does this step make sense for your team at this time? How will it help you move forward as a group?

Source: Adapted from Ferriter, W. M., Graham, P., & Wight, M. (2013). Making teamwork meaningful: Leading progress-driven collaboration in a PLC. *Bloomington, IN: Solution Tree Press.*

Additional Resources
Strengthening the Collegial Practices of Learning Teams

Survey: The Trust on Your Learning Team

Instructions: This survey is designed to collect information about the levels of trust on your learning team. For the following descriptors, please indicate (1) the extent to which you agree or disagree with each statement by circling one of the three letters on the left-hand side, and (2) the level of importance that you place on each indicator by circling one of the three numbers on the right-hand side.

D = Disagree, N = Neutral, A = Agree   1 = Very important, 2 = Somewhat important, 3 = Not important

My colleagues willingly share their materials, resources, and ideas with me.	D	N	A	1	2	3
I feel welcome in my colleagues' classrooms before and after school.	D	N	A	1	2	3
I feel welcome in my colleagues' classrooms during their instructional periods.	D	N	A	1	2	3
I feel comfortable with my colleagues in my room during my instructional periods.	D	N	A	1	2	3
I believe that my colleagues have good intentions in their interactions with me.	D	N	A	1	2	3
I believe that my colleagues have good intentions in their interactions with students.	D	N	A	1	2	3
I know that I can count on my colleagues.	D	N	A	1	2	3
I believe that my colleagues are honest.	D	N	A	1	2	3
I am not afraid to share student learning results with my colleagues.	D	N	A	1	2	3
I believe that my colleagues are competent and capable teachers.	D	N	A	1	2	3
I believe that I can learn from my colleagues.	D	N	A	1	2	3
I believe that everyone on my team makes meaningful contributions to our work.	D	N	A	1	2	3
I believe that everyone on my team is pulling in the same direction.	D	N	A	1	2	3
Our team celebrates the personal and professional successes of individual members.	D	N	A	1	2	3
Our team celebrates our collective accomplishments.	D	N	A	1	2	3
I look forward to the time that I spend with my colleagues.	D	N	A	1	2	3

Final Thoughts: On the back of this page, please describe the kind of support you think your team would need in order to improve the overall levels of trust between teachers.

Source: Graham, P., & Ferriter, W. M. (2010). Building a Professional Learning Community at Work: A guide to the first year. Bloomington, IN: Solution Tree Press.

2

What Do We Want Students to Learn?

In his seminal text *What Works in Schools: Translating Research Into Action*, education researcher Robert J. Marzano (2003) identifies the creation of a guaranteed and viable curriculum (GVC) as the school-based factor likely to have the greatest impact on student achievement. For Marzano (2003), a *guaranteed curriculum* is one that all students at the same grade level and in the same school have access to. A *viable curriculum* is a curriculum that can realistically be taught to—and learned by—students in the time available for learning. "At its essence, a GVC represents the core non-negotiables of student learning. It's what schools and teachers commit to providing for all students," explains Kathleen Dempsey (2017), the director of the North Central Comprehensive Center at McREL International.

The concept of creating a guaranteed and viable curriculum originated with research in the 1960s that raised questions about whether all students had the same *opportunity* to learn essential concepts and skills in schools, and then suggested that the performance of individual students might have more to do with the teaching that they had been exposed to than it did with the academic ability of the learner (Marzano, 2003). Recommendations found in *A Nation at Risk* (National Commission on Excellence in Education, 1983)—a research report that forever changed American schooling—magnified this problem. As they raced to meet the report's challenge to adopt more rigorous and measurable standards, states created curriculum documents that included far more content than could realistically be covered during a single school year (as cited in Marzano, 2003). Teachers responded by making individual choices about which standards they were going to cover and which they were going to omit during a school year, creating even greater disparities between what students in different classrooms in the exact same hallways were being exposed to.

Developing and Delivering a Guaranteed and Viable Curriculum

Creating a guaranteed and viable curriculum in a PLC at Work starts when teams answer the first critical question of learning together: What is it that we want our students to learn? (DuFour et al., 2016). To answer this question, collaborative teams work together to identify *need to knows* and *nice to knows* for every unit that they teach during a school year. *Need to knows* are small sets of concepts and skills that every student must master in order to be successful. *Nice to knows* are concepts and skills that are important, but not essential for students to master before moving to the next grade level. Teams also make general pacing decisions while determining what they want students to learn, settling on a logical sequence for introducing students to essential skills and concepts, and estimating the amount of time necessary for students to master each essential skill or concept.

Students benefit when their teachers answer the first critical question of learning in a PLC at Work together because doing so eliminates opportunity gaps. When implemented with fidelity, a guaranteed and viable curriculum ensures that every student, regardless of teacher, has access to knowledge and skills essential for continued success. Teachers benefit from answering the first critical question of learning in a PLC at Work together because they gain access to the professional expertise of their peers. No longer are they forced to make important decisions about what students need to know and be able to do on their own. Instead, their core beliefs about the essentials in their curriculum are confirmed or challenged by peers with different experiences. Each conversation tied to the first critical question of learning becomes a new opportunity for teachers to discover more about the content that they are required to teach.

Finally, answering the first critical question of learning in a PLC at Work can provide teams with the clarity, precision, and focus necessary for producing real results together (Saphier, 2005). Studying the impact of professional practice for *every* concept and skill listed in state and district curriculum materials is simply impossible given the limited amount of collaborative time available to learning teams in most districts. The solution is to use the knowledge and expertise of teachers, combined with evidence gleaned from data sources documenting student performance, to explicitly structure collective inquiry around a smaller handful of concepts and skills that matter the most.

Resources for What We Want Students to Learn

The resources in this chapter are all designed to help your learning team build a guaranteed and viable curriculum together. The five fundamentals for determining what you want students to learn include the following.

1. **"Checklist: Identifying Essential Learning Outcomes for a Unit of Study"** (page 55)—The first step that any learning team must take to ensure that it is delivering a guaranteed and viable curriculum is to collectively reflect on the skills, knowledge, and dispositions—that is, academic behaviors—that students are expected to master by the end of a unit of instruction. Your team can use this checklist, combined with evidence from school, district, and state performance assessments, to identify and prioritize a manageable set of essential learning outcomes for each unit of study.

2. **"Tool: Unpacking Essential Standards"** (pages 56–57)—Working together to break down essential standards into student-friendly learning targets can help teachers on collaborative teams build a shared understanding of the concepts and skills that students are expected to master, and develop a clear language for communicating those standards to the students in their classrooms. Use this template to begin unpacking an essential standard that you are responsible for teaching. This tool is followed on page 58 by a sample designed to help you see how it can be used.

3. **"Tool: Pacing Guide for a Cycle of Instruction"** (pages 60–61)—Collaborative teams constantly work through short cycles of planning, instruction, assessment, and action. Each cycle centers on three to five essential outcomes that can be taught in approximately fifteen to twenty days. Most importantly, each cycle ends with a common formative assessment that you can use to take next steps together. Use this template to plan your next short cycle of instruction. This tool is followed on page 62 by a sample designed to help you see how it can be used.

4. **"Tool: Developing Exemplars to Standardize Expectations"** (page 64)—Developing a guaranteed and viable curriculum isn't just a matter of identifying essential standards for a unit of study. It also involves standardizing expectations for what mastery looks like in action. To standardize teacher expectations and to communicate expectations to both parents and students, teams must work together to develop sets of exemplars representing different levels of student performance on each learning target. Use this template to develop a set of exemplars for one of your upcoming learning targets. This tool is followed on pages 65–68 by two samples designed to help you see how it can be used. They represent two different levels of performance on the same task. A complete set of exemplars would include four team-developed samples representing the levels of performance detailed on the tool.

5. **"Tool: SMART Goal Worksheet"** (page 69)—Another step that collaborative teams take to structure their work is developing an annual SMART goal. SMART goals are strategic and specific, measurable, attainable, results

oriented, and time bound, and they keep teams focused on moving forward together over the course of a school year (Conzemius & O'Neill, 2014). Use this template to write a SMART goal to lend focus to the work of your learning team. This tool is followed on pages 70–74 by samples that are designed to help you see how it can be used.

The following are additional resources for determining what you want students to learn.

- **"Tool: Essential Standards Chart"** (pages 76–77)—In *Simplifying Response to Intervention*, collaboration experts Austin Buffum, Mike Mattos, and Chris Weber (2012) argue that teams should use Essential Standards Charts to articulate the guaranteed and viable curriculum for every unit. This template from *Simplifying Response to Intervention* (Buffum et al., 2012), which is different in format from but similar in content to the "Pacing Guide for a Unit of Instruction" found in the five fundamentals for this chapter, can help you do just that. It is followed on page 78 by a sample designed to help you see how it can be used.

- **"Tool: Identifying Important Questions to Study Together"** (page 80)—Richard DuFour argues that collaborative teams "work together collaboratively in recurring cycles of collective inquiry and action research to achieve better results for the students they serve" (as cited in Marzano, Warrick, Rains, & DuFour, 2018, p. 2). Determining what to focus on during these cycles of inquiry starts by identifying questions that pass the endurance, leverage, and readiness test (Reeves, 2002). Use this template to help your team brainstorm potential research questions that are worth studying together. A protocol follows on page 81 to help take you through the process of using this template.

- **"Tool: Spotting Patterns in Standardized Tests and Universal Screening Data"** (pages 83–84)—Collaborative teams recognize that they can glean valuable information on the concepts and skills that students are struggling with from standardized test and universal screening data collected at the school level. Sometimes the best way to identify these concepts and skills is to take advantage of the expertise of professionals working beyond the classroom who have greater access to—and more familiarity with—these data sets. Use this template to gather and reflect on student learning patterns spotted by these professionals.

- **"Tool: Helping Singletons Identify Academic Skills and Dispositions Worth Studying"** (pages 85–86)—For singletons in a PLC at Work, identifying essential outcomes worth studying in recurring cycles of collective inquiry can feel impossible. After all, collaboration is often centered on content covered in a common curriculum—something that singletons rarely share with their collaborative partners. But if teams are willing to think beyond the required curriculum, they can find all kinds of academic skills and dispositions necessary for being successful that are worth studying together. If you are working on a team of singletons, use the six research-based lists of essential academic skills and dispositions and the reflection questions listed in this template to identify a collaborative focus for your learning team.

■ **"Tool: Helping Singletons Identify Essential Outcomes to Study"** (page 87)—Regardless of composition, collaborative teams engage in ongoing cycles of inquiry around their practice. For grade-level or subject-specific teams, shared curriculum often stands at the center of those cycles of inquiry. Teams that comprise members who are the only teacher of their subject or their grade level, however, often must look beyond their curriculum to identify an area of focus for collective cycles of inquiry. If you are a singleton or a teacher in a small school, use this template with your team to begin shaping your cycle of inquiry together.

■ **"Survey: Does Your Team Have a Guaranteed and Viable Curriculum?"** (pages 88–89)—Success for students depends on learning teams working together to determine a guaranteed and viable curriculum for their classes. A *guaranteed curriculum* is one that *every* teacher agrees to teach. A *viable curriculum* is a curriculum that is deliverable in the time that teachers spend with their students. Use this survey to rate your team's work toward creating a guaranteed and viable curriculum for your students.

■ **"Tool: Guaranteed and Viable Curriculum Reflection Questions"** (page 90)—One of the first steps that you must take in order to leverage the power of a guaranteed and viable curriculum is to convince already busy teachers that developing lists of shared outcomes is worth the time and energy. Use the questions included on this template to start that conversation with members of your learning team.

Five Fundamental Resources

for What We Want Students to Learn

Checklist: Identifying Essential Learning Outcomes for a Unit of Study

Instructions: As a team, consult state and district curriculum guides for potential essential outcomes for an upcoming unit of study. Compile the outcomes that your team members think might be essential, and then complete one checklist for each of the outcomes to determine if it should be added to your team's list of essentials for your next unit of study.

Name of Unit:		
Required Content and Skill Objective Under Consideration		
Does this essential learning outcome directly support the mission of our school and our shared vision of quality instruction?	Yes	No
Does this essential learning outcome cover knowledge or skills that will be new to our students, valuable to their continued studies, or important long after they have left school?	Yes	No
Is there any evidence in school curriculum guides that our students have *been exposed to* this essential learning outcome in previous years?	Yes	No
Is there any evidence in recent assessments that our students have *mastered* this essential learning outcome in previous years?	Yes	No
Is there any evidence in recent assessments that our students have *struggled to master* this essential learning outcome in previous years?	Yes	No
Will mastering this essential learning outcome help our students *excel in* other content areas or grade levels? If so, which ones?	Yes	No
Would you recommend that we include this learning outcome on our list of essential learning outcomes for this unit?	Yes	No
Final Thoughts on This Learning Outcome		

Tool: Unpacking Essential Standards

Step 1: Annotate the Essential Standard

Instructions: Using a process adapted from the work of Larry Ainsworth (2003) by education leadership consultants Kim Bailey and Chris Jakicic (2019), annotate one of your essential standards in the following box. Begin by circling verbs (skills students should master), then underline nouns (concepts or facts students should master) and put brackets around words that show the context of the task students will perform to demonstrate mastery.

Step 2: Reflect on the Standard

Instructions: Answer the following questions about the essential standard that you annotated in step 1.

Using your annotations, list the content knowledge that students will need to know in order to master this standard.	
Using your annotations, list the skills that students will need to demonstrate in order to master this standard.	
Why is it important for students to master this standard?	
How can you assess the progress that students are making toward mastering this standard?	

Step 3: Write Student-Friendly Learning Targets

Instructions: Create a set of three to five statements describing exactly what students will need to know and be able to do in order to master this standard. Remember to write your learning targets in student-friendly language so that you can effectively communicate your expectations to your students. Also, remember to include a "doing task" that students can complete in order to demonstrate mastery of the learning target.

Expected Learning	Expected Learning in Student-Friendly Language	Doing Task
Sample: Students will need to understand that poets often use figurative language to create a mood or tone for their poems.	*Sample:* I can explain how writers use figurative language to influence readers' interpretations.	*Sample:* This means that I can look at similes, metaphors, and personification in poems and make a prediction about how they might make readers feel.

Five Fundamental Resources — What We Want Students to Learn

References

Ainsworth, L. (2003). *"Unwrapping" the standards: A simple process to make standards manageable.* Englewood, CO: Advanced Learning Press.

Bailey, K., & Jakicic, C. (2019). *Make it happen: Coaching with the four critical questions of PLCs at Work.* Bloomington, IN: Solution Tree Press.

Sample: Unpacking Essential Standards—Kindergarten

Step 1: Annotate the Essential Standard

Instructions: Using a process adapted from the work of Larry Ainsworth (2003) by education leadership consultants Kim Bailey and Chris Jakicic (2019), annotate one of your essential standards in the following box. Begin by circling verbs (skills students should master), then underline nouns (concepts or facts students should master) and put brackets around words that show the context of the task students will perform to demonstrate mastery.

Essential Standard to Unpack:
Participate in collaborative conversations with diverse partners about kindergarten topics and texts with peers and adults in small and larger groups.
Annotated Essential Standard:
(Participate in collaborative conversations) [with diverse partners] <u>about kindergarten topics and texts</u> [with peers and adults in small and larger groups].

Step 2: Reflect on the Standard

Instructions: Answer the following questions about the essential standard that you annotated in step 1.

Using your annotations, list the content knowledge that students will need to know in order to master this standard.	This is open for our interpretation. The only requirements are that we use both kindergarten topics and kindergarten texts in the conversations that we create. Participating in a conversation on a topic is probably going to be easier for our students than participating in a conversation on a text.
Using your annotations, list the skills that students will need to demonstrate in order to master this standard.	For kindergartners, we think "participating in a collaborative conversation" will include things like adding original ideas, asking important questions, and being a good listener. Our advanced students may be able to build on the ideas of others by agreeing and disagreeing with thoughts that they hear.
Why is it important for students to master this standard?	Collaborative dialogue is essential for knowledge building. It is also an important skill for today simply because our students are surrounded by lots of examples of unhealthy discourse and disagreement.
How can you assess the progress that students are making toward mastering this standard?	We are going to need to make a rubric or a checklist detailing the kinds of behaviors that we hope to see from students in collaborative conversations. Then, we can use that rubric when watching students participate in both small- and large-group conversations.

page 1 of 2

Step 3: Write Student-Friendly Learning Targets

Instructions: Create a set of three to five statements describing exactly what students will need to know and be able to do in order to master this standard. Remember to write your learning targets in student-friendly language so that you can effectively communicate your expectations to your students. Also, remember to include a "doing task" that students can complete in order to demonstrate mastery of the learning target.

Expected Learning	Expected Learning in Student-Friendly Language	Doing Task
Students need to be able to add original ideas to collaborative conversations.	I can add new ideas when participating in a conversation with my peers.	This means I can make a list of three important ideas that I would like to share in a classroom conversation and choose one to share while we are talking with one another.
Students need to be able to ask good questions in order to participate in collaborative conversations.	I can ask a good question when participating in a conversation with my peers.	This means I can make a list of three questions that I would like to ask in a classroom conversation and choose one to share while we are talking with one another.
Students need to be able to respond to the ideas that they are hearing in a collaborative conversation.	I can respond to something that I have heard when participating in a conversation with my peers.	This means I can use the phrases "I agree with _____ because . . .," "I disagree with _____ because . . .," or "I'm not sure about _____ because . . ." at least once the next time that we are talking with one another.

References

Ainsworth, L. (2003). *"Unwrapping" the standards: A simple process to make standards manageable.* Englewood, CO: Advanced Learning Press.

Bailey, K., & Jakicic, C. (2019). *Make it happen: Coaching with the four critical questions of PLCs at Work.* Bloomington, IN: Solution Tree Press.

Five Fundamental Resources: What We Want Students to Learn

The Big Book of Tools for Collaborative Teams in a PLC at Work © 2020 Solution Tree Press • SolutionTree.com
Visit **go.SolutionTree.com/PLCbooks/BBTCT** and enter the unique access code found on the book's inside front cover to access this reproducible.

Tool: Pacing Guide for a Cycle of Instruction

Instructions: In the first column, list sequentially three to five essential outcomes you will cover in this cycle of instruction and use Webb's (1997) Depth of Knowledge (DOK) matrix to identify the level of rigor that each one requires. Then, in the second column, estimate the number of lessons it will take to teach each outcome to mastery. Remember that cycles of instruction should happen quickly in a professional learning community, taking roughly fifteen to twenty instructional days to complete. For the third column, answer these questions: What should every student know and be able to do when we are finished teaching this outcome? What skills should they be able to demonstrate? What vocabulary should they know? In the last column, record the instructional activities you are going to use to teach these concepts to the students in your classes. Finally, fill in the date and requirements for the common formative assessment that will cover this unit.

Name of Unit: _____

Number of Weeks Necessary for Teaching the Outcomes in This Cycle of Instruction: _____

Dates for This Cycle of Instruction:

Essential Outcomes	Estimated Pacing	Knowledge, Skills, and Vocabulary to Cover	Core Instructional Activities
DOK Level of Target: ☐ Recall and Reproduction ☐ Skills and Concepts ☐ Strategic Thinking ☐ Extended Thinking			
DOK Level of Target: ☐ Recall and Reproduction ☐ Skills and Concepts ☐ Strategic Thinking ☐ Extended Thinking			
DOK Level of Target: ☐ Recall and Reproduction ☐ Skills and Concepts ☐ Strategic Thinking ☐ Extended Thinking			

DOK Level of Target: ☐ Recall and Reproduction ☐ Skills and Concepts ☐ Strategic Thinking ☐ Extended Thinking		
DOK Level of Target: ☐ Recall and Reproduction ☐ Skills and Concepts ☐ Strategic Thinking ☐ Extended Thinking		

Date of Common Formative Assessment:

Requirements for Common Formative Assessments:

List assessments here, including where they are stored and any materials necessary to administer them. Remember that a good common formative assessment only covers three to five concepts. Also, remember that it is important to ask three to five questions per concept on your common formative assessment in order to gather enough data to take action.

Reference

Webb, N. L. (1997). *Research monograph number 6: Criteria for alignment of expectations and assessments in mathematics and science education.* Washington, DC: Council of Chief State School Officers.

Five Fundamental Resources — What We Want Students to Learn

Sample: Pacing Guide for a Cycle of Instruction

Instructions: In the first column, list sequentially three to five essential outcomes you will cover in this cycle of instruction and use Webb's (1997) Depth of Knowledge (DOK) matrix to identify the level of rigor that each one requires. Then, in the second column, estimate the number of lessons it will take to teach each outcome to mastery. Remember that cycles of instruction should happen quickly in a professional learning community, taking roughly fifteen to twenty instructional days to complete. For the third column, answer these questions: What should every student know and be able to do when we are finished teaching this outcome? What skills should they be able to demonstrate? What vocabulary should they know? In the last column, record the instructional activities you are going to use to teach these concepts to the students in your classes. Finally, fill in the date and requirements for the common formative assessment that will cover this unit.

Name of Unit: Matter

Number of Weeks Necessary for Teaching the Outcomes in This Cycle of Instruction: Four Weeks

Dates for This Cycle of Instruction: Monday, October 29, to Friday, November 2

Essential Outcomes	Estimated Pacing	Knowledge, Skills, and Vocabulary to Cover	Core Instructional Activities
Measuring Matter **DOK Level of Target:** ☐ Recall and Reproduction ☑ Skills and Concepts ☐ Strategic Thinking ☐ Extended Thinking	Two class periods	Students should understand the difference between *mass* and *volume*. Students should understand how mass and volume work together to determine the *density* of a substance. Students will learn to use a *triple beam balance* to measure the mass of an object. Students should understand how to calculate the volume of an *irregular solid* using a *graduated cylinder* and the *displacement of water*.	Activity: What *Is* the Density of Your Silent Reading Book? Activity: Archimedes and the Golden Crown
Density's Role in Floating and Sinking **DOK Level of Target:** ☐ Recall and Reproduction ☐ Skills and Concepts ☑ Strategic Thinking ☐ Extended Thinking	Two class periods	Students should understand that dense materials will always *push through* less dense materials. Students should understand that you can't determine the density of an object just by the size of an object. Instead, density of an object is a function of the relationship between the size of an object and the mass inside of it.	Activity: Get in the Game With Team Density

Five Fundamental Resources
What We Want Students to Learn

| Density as a Characteristic Property of Matter

DOK Level of Target:
☑ Recall and Reproduction
☐ Skills and Concepts
☐ Strategic Thinking
☐ Extended Thinking | One class period | Students should understand that *characteristic properties of matter* don't change no matter how much of a substance you have. That makes those properties useful for identifying unknown substances.

Students should understand that density is a characteristic property of matter.

Students should understand that mass and volume are not characteristic properties of matter. They are both dependent on the amount of a substance that you have. | Activity: How Dense *Is* That Modeling Clay? |

Date of Common Formative Assessment:

Monday, November 5

Requirements for Common Formative Assessments:

List assessments here, including where they are stored and any materials necessary to administer them. Remember that a good common formative assessment only covers three to five concepts. Also, remember that it is important to ask three to five questions per concept on your common formative assessment in order to gather enough data to take action.

- **Selected-Response Assessment: Measuring Matter and Understanding Density**—*The assessment is written and stored in our team drive. Mastery = 70 percent or higher*

- **Performance Assessment: Calculating the Density of a Marble**—*Hand each group of two students a marble and ask them to calculate its density. Students should be able to use a triple beam balance to calculate the mass and apply the displacement of water method to determine its volume. A checklist for scoring this performance is stored in our team drive.*

Reference

Webb, N. L. (1997). *Research monograph number 6: Criteria for alignment of expectations and assessments in mathematics and science education*. Washington, DC: Council of Chief State School Officers.

Tool: Developing Exemplars to Standardize Expectations

Instructions: Describe the task that all students will be asked to complete as a demonstration of mastery in the first row. Then, in the second row, describe the learning target you are assessing with this task. In the left column, fill in the exemplar that your team has generated to spotlight common patterns present in student responses at this level of performance. In the right column, add teacher comments: reasons that this exemplar accurately represents responses at this level of performance. Finally, in the last row, write a one- to two-sentence summary of the characteristics of responses that demonstrate this level of performance. Remember to use student-friendly language throughout your exemplars. Doing so will make your final products more useful to your learners.

Task Students Will Complete or Question Students Will Answer to Demonstrate Mastery:

Learning Target This Task Is Designed to Assess:

Level of Performance Demonstrated by This Exemplar
(Circle one.)

Beginning	Developing	Mastering	Exceeding
Exemplar		**Teacher Comments**	

Defining Characteristics of Responses Demonstrating This Level of Performance

Sample 1: Developing Exemplars to Standardize Expectations—High School Social Studies

Instructions: Describe the task that all students will be asked to complete as a demonstration of mastery in the first row. Then, in the second row, describe the learning target you are assessing with this task. In the left column, fill in the exemplar that your team has generated to spotlight common patterns present in student responses at this level of performance. In the right column, add teacher comments: reasons that this exemplar accurately represents responses at this level of performance. Finally, in the last row, write a one- to two-sentence summary of the characteristics of responses that demonstrate this level of performance. Remember to use student-friendly language throughout your exemplars. Doing so will make your final products more useful to your learners.

Exemplar: Exceeding

Task Students Will Complete or Question Students Will Answer to Demonstrate Mastery:
High School Social Studies: Gap Thinking—Take a Position on an Important Current Event
In this task, students are asked to take a position on any important current event. Then, students are asked to identify additional information that they would need to know to ensure that their position is responsible. We call this work *identifying gaps in your own thinking* and it ties into Dimension 4, "Communicating Conclusions and Taking Informed Action," of the C3 (College, Career, and Civic Life) Framework for Social Studies State Standards (National Council for the Social Studies, n.d.).
This exemplar is taken from a task where students were asked to think through their position on the confrontation that occurred on the steps of the Lincoln Memorial on January 18, 2019, between a group of teens from Covington Catholic High School on a school field trip and a Native American activist. Students were asked, "Were the Covington Catholic students in the wrong during their confrontation with Native American activist Nathan Phillips?"

Learning Target This Task Is Designed to Assess:
I understand the role that questioning my own thinking can play in taking informed action. This means I can take a position on an important current event and identify gaps in my thinking that make it difficult to ensure that my position is responsible.

Level of Performance Demonstrated by This Exemplar
(Circle one.)

Beginning	Developing	Mastering	Exceeding

Exemplar	Teacher Comments
I think that the Covington Catholic students *were* in the wrong during their interaction with Native American activist Nathan Phillips. They surrounded Mr. Phillips in a way that would be perceived by anyone as intimidating. They also joined in group chants that were designed to mock him and his heritage. I also think the students knew they were wrong. Several seemed to be nervously laughing and joining in only out of peer pressure. I only do that when I know that what I am doing is something I shouldn't be doing.	• Student response is on topic and shows evidence of attempts to apply the content we have been studying in class to both his position and the gaps in thinking. • Student includes at least two gaps in thinking that are clearly connected to the question under study and to the student's original position.

Five Fundamental Resources
What We Want Students to Learn

Exemplar	Teacher Comments
But I'm not sure because:	• Gaps in thinking show extensive reflection about the topic being studied.
• I don't know the biases or positions of the people who took the videos that I have seen. Those biases may change what they show in their videos.	• There is no question that if this student had more detail about the gaps in his thinking, he would be able to craft a more responsible position and to take a more informed action.
• I'm not sure that I have seen the entire confrontation yet. The videos that I have watched all seem to start in the middle of the confrontation.	
• I haven't heard from any of the parents or teachers who were on the trip. Their perspective might change my mind about the event.	
• I haven't heard from any other neutral observers of the event. I've only heard from people directly involved in the event—and they are the most likely to be biased.	

Defining Characteristics of Responses Demonstrating This Level of Performance
Student responses that exceed expectations have a very clear connection between the position that you originally took and the gaps in thinking that you have identified. You exceed expectations when you demonstrate that finding answers to your gaps in thinking would help you take a more informed action or develop a more responsible position.

(Sidebar, left margin:) **Five Fundamental Resources** What We Want Students to Learn

Reference

National Council for the Social Studies. (n.d.). *The college, career, and civic life (C3) framework for social studies state standards: Guidance for enhancing the rigor of K–12 civics, economics, geography, and history.* Accessed at www.social studies.org/sites/default/files/c3/C3-Framework-for-Social-Studies.pdf on October 7, 2019.

Sample 2: Developing Exemplars to Standardize Expectations—High School Social Studies

Instructions: Describe the task that all students will be asked to complete as a demonstration of mastery in the first row. Then, in the second row, describe the learning target you are assessing with this task. In the left column, fill in the exemplar that your team has generated to spotlight common patterns present in student responses at this level of performance. In the right column, add teacher comments: reasons that this exemplar accurately represents responses at this level of performance. Finally, in the last row, write a one- to two-sentence summary of the characteristics of responses that demonstrate this level of performance. Remember to use student-friendly language throughout your exemplars. Doing so will make your final products more useful to your learners.

Exemplar: Developing

<table>
<tr><td colspan="2">Task Students Will Complete or Question Students Will Answer to Demonstrate Mastery:

High School Social Studies: Gap Thinking—Take a Position on an Important Current Event

In this task, students are asked to take a position on any important current event. Then, students are asked to identify additional information that they would need to know to ensure that their position is responsible. We call this work identifying gaps in your own thinking and it ties into Dimension 4, "Communicating Conclusions and Taking Informed Action," of the C3 (College, Career, and Civic Life) Framework for Social Studies State Standards (National Council for the Social Studies, n.d.).

This exemplar is taken from a task where students were asked to think through their position on the confrontation that occurred on the steps of the Lincoln Memorial on January 18, 2019, between a group of teens from Covington Catholic High School on a school field trip and a Native American activist. Students were asked, "Were the Covington Catholic students in the wrong during their confrontation with Native American activist Nathan Phillips?"</td></tr>
<tr><td colspan="2">Learning Target This Task Is Designed to Assess:

I understand the role that questioning my own thinking can play in taking informed action. This means I can take a position on an important current event and identify gaps in my thinking that make it difficult to ensure that my position is responsible.</td></tr>
<tr><td colspan="2">Level of Performance Demonstrated by This Exemplar
(Circle one.)</td></tr>
<tr><td>Beginning</td><td>(Developing)   Mastering   Exceeding</td></tr>
<tr><td>Exemplar</td><td>Teacher Comments</td></tr>
<tr><td>I think that the Covington Catholic students were not in the wrong during their interaction with Native American activist Nathan Phillips. They were just acting like ordinary high school kids. In fact, I think Nathan Phillips started the whole thing.

But I'm not sure because:

• I don't know very much about Native Americans.

• I don't go to a private school like Covington Catholic.

• I have never been to Washington, DC.</td><td>• Student has attempted a response to the question, taken a position, and included gaps in thinking.

• Gaps in thinking, however, are not clearly connected to the question, the current event under study, or the position taken by the student.

• Gaps in thinking may also be too broad, too vague, or too simple, or student may be expressing an opinion about the current event instead of recognizing a gap in knowledge.

• Having more detail about the gaps in thinking the student has identified would not leave the student better prepared to craft a more responsible position or to take more informed action.

• Writing is unclear and hard to follow.</td></tr>
</table>

page 1 of 2

The Big Book of Tools for Collaborative Teams in a PLC at Work © 2020 Solution Tree Press • SolutionTree.com

Visit **go.SolutionTree.com/PLCbooks/BBTCT** and enter the unique access code found on the book's inside front cover to access this reproducible.

Defining Characteristics of Responses Demonstrating This Level of Performance
In a response that is developing, I can tell that you are thinking about the right current event. You have also clearly stated your position on the current event. However, it is difficult to see any clear connection between your gaps in thinking and the position that you are taking. Having more detail about your gaps in thinking would give you more information about the current event, but that information wouldn't help you take more informed action.

Reference

National Council for the Social Studies. (n.d.). *The college, career, and civic life (C3) framework for social studies state standards: Guidance for enhancing the rigor of K–12 civics, economics, geography, and history.* Accessed at www.social studies.org/sites/default/files/c3/C3-Framework-for-Social-Studies.pdf on October 7, 2019.

Tool: SMART Goal Worksheet

School:

Team Members:

District Goal(s):

School Goal(s):

Team Name:

Team Leader:

Team SMART Goal	Strategies and Action Steps	Who Is Responsible	Target Date or Timeline	Evidence of Effectiveness

Source: DuFour, R., DuFour, R., Eaker, R., Many, T. W., & Mattos, M. (2016). Learning by doing: A handbook for Professional Learning Communities at Work (3rd ed.). Bloomington, IN: Solution Tree Press.

Five Fundamental Resources
What We Want Students to Learn

page 1 of 3

Sample: SMART Goal Worksheet—Third-Grade Team

School: George Washington Elementary   **Team Name:** Third Grade   **Team Leader:** Theresa Smith

Team Members: Ken Thomas, Joe Ramirez, Cathy Armstrong, Amy Wu

District Goal(s):

- We will increase student achievement and close the achievement gap in all areas using a variety of indicators to document improved learning on the part of our students.

School Goal(s):

- We will improve student achievement in language arts as measured by local, district, state, and national indicators.

Team SMART Goal	Strategies and Action Steps	Who Is Responsible	Target Date or Timeline	Evidence of Effectiveness
Our Current Reality: Last year, 85 percent of our students met or exceeded the target score of 3 on our state's writing prompt in May. **Our SMART Goal:** This year, at least 90 percent of our students will meet or exceed the target score of 3 on our state's writing prompt in May.	**Curriculum** 1. Clarify and pace essential student learning outcomes in writing using standards documents, curriculum guides, assessment blueprints and data, and the wish list of skills from the fourth-grade team.	All members of our team	October 15	Lists of essential student learning outcomes and pacing guide Increased results for all students on team, district, state, and national indicators

Assessments

Task	Who	When	Evidence
2. Develop, implement, and collaboratively score grade-level formative writing prompts to: a. Frequently monitor each student's learning of essential writing outcomes b. Provide students with multiple opportunities to demonstrate progress in meeting and exceeding learning targets in writing c. Learn with and from each other better ways to help students become proficient writers	All members of our team	October–May Checkpoints at midpoint of each grading period District benchmark assessments at end of each semester	Common writing prompts Common writing rubric Increased results for all students on team, district, state, and national indicators
3. Provide students with writing assignments in all subject areas, and utilize a variety of instructional strategies to help students learn all essential writing skills.	All members of our team Principal Resource staff Volunteers	Daily, September–May	Intervention/enrichment schedule Student learning results
4. Initiate individual and small-group sessions to provide additional intervention and enrichment focused on writing.	All members of our team	Daily, September–May	Intervention/enrichment schedule Student learning results

Team SMART Goal	Strategies and Action Steps	Who Is Responsible	Target Date or Timeline	Evidence of Effectiveness
	5. Provide parents with resources and strategies to help their children succeed as writers.	All members of our team	First semester workshop: 10/20 Second semester workshop: 1/19 Newsletters End-of-grading-period conferences	Number of parents in attendance Study guides and newsletters
	Staff Development 6. Develop, implement, and evaluate our team action research project in writing to improve our individual and collective ability to help our students learn to write at high levels. Use information from our common formative assessments to identify staff development needs and engage in ongoing, job-embedded staff development in the area of writing.	All members of our team	Weekly collaborative team meetings Staff development days Faculty meeting sessions Additional professional learning time by request	Common assessments Quarterly reviews Midyear progress reports End-of-year team evaluations Increased results for all students on team, district, state, and national indicators

Source: DuFour, R., DuFour, R., Eaker, R., Many, T. W., & Mattos, M. (2016). Learning by doing: A handbook for Professional Learning Communities at Work (3rd ed.). Bloomington, IN: Solution Tree Press.

Sample: SMART Goal Worksheet—American Government

School: John Adams High School **Team Name:** American Government **Team Leader:** Tom Botimer

Team Members: Dan Hahn, Andy Bradford, Nick Larsen, Helen Harvey

District Goal(s):

1. We will increase student achievement and close the achievement gap in all areas using a variety of indicators to document improved learning on the part of our students.

2. We will provide more students with access to our most rigorous curriculum in each subject area and grade level.

School Goal(s): We will increase by at least 10 percent the number of students earning credit in—

1. Advanced placement courses

2. Capstone courses in a departmental sequence

Team SMART Goal	Strategies and Action Steps	Who Is Responsible	Target Date or Timeline	Evidence of Effectiveness
Our Current Reality: All students must complete a semester of American Government as a graduation requirement. Last year, only 10 percent of the graduating class fulfilled that requirement by enrolling in advanced placement (AP) American Government.	We will make a presentation in each section of United States History, encouraging students to enroll in AP American Government and listing the advantages for doing so.	The team leader will coordinate the schedule for these presentations with the team leader for United States History. Each member of the team will assist in making these presentations and will distribute a written list of advantages created by the team.	Presentations will be completed by the end of January prior to students registering for their courses for next year.	The presentation has been made in every United States History class.

Five Fundamental Resources
What We Want Students to Learn

Team SMART Goal	Strategies and Action Steps	Who Is Responsible	Target Date or Timeline	Evidence of Effectiveness
Our SMART Goal: At least 20 percent of the current junior class will enroll in advanced placement American Government and earn a score of 3, 4, or 5 on the advanced placement American Government exam by the end of next school year.	We will coordinate with the guidance department to ensure that when counselors register students for classes, they encourage any student who receives an A at the end of the first semester of United States History to enroll in AP American Government.	The team leader will attend the counselors' team meeting to enlist their support, explain advantages of the AP program, and share the team's strategies for supporting students in AP American Government.	End of the first semester	Minutes of meeting
	We will advise parents of the benefits of AP American Government.	The team will draft a letter to parents of students who earn an A in United States History at the end of the semester. The letter will list the advantages of completing this course while in high school for any student planning on attending college. It will also include the team's strategy to provide students with additional support. The team will also create a flyer on the benefits of the AP program to be distributed during parent open house.	The flyer will be created for distribution at the open house in early October. The letter will be sent at the end of the first semester.	Completed documents
	We will create study groups to review material prior to the comprehensive assessments we administer every six weeks.	The team will create the common comprehensive assessments. Each member will be responsible for conducting one study group to help students review for these tests. Study groups will be held on three evenings in the week prior to the test.	Ongoing throughout the semester	Completion of common assessments and student performance on common assessments The number of students earning honor grades on the AP exam in American Government will double last year's total.

Source: DuFour, R., DuFour, R., Eaker, R., Many, T. W., & Mattos, M. (2016). Learning by doing: A handbook for Professional Learning Communities at Work (3rd ed.). Bloomington, IN: Solution Tree Press.

Additional Resources

for What We Want Students to Learn

Tool: Essential Standards Chart

What Is It We Expect Students to Learn?					
Grade:		Subject:		Semester:	Team Members:
Description of Standard	**Example of Rigor**	**Prerequisite Skills**	**When Taught**	**Common Summative Assessment**	**Extension Standards**
What is the essential standard to be learned? Describe in student-friendly vocabulary.	What does proficient student work look like? Provide an example and/or description.	What prior knowledge, skills, and/or vocabulary are needed for a student to master this standard?	When will this standard be taught?	What assessment(s) will be used to measure student mastery?	What will we do when students have already learned this standard?

Working in collaborative teams, examine all relevant documents, Common Core standards, state standards, and district power standards, and then apply the criteria of endurance, leverage, and readiness to determine which standards are essential for all students to master. Remember, less is more. For each standard selected, complete the remaining columns. Complete this chart by the second or third week of each instructional period (semester).

Source: Buffum, A., Mattos, M., & Weber, C. (2012). Simplifying response to intervention: Four essential guiding principles. Bloomington, IN: Solution Tree Press.

page 2 of 2

Additional Resources
What We Want Students to Learn

Sample: Essential Standards Chart—Second-Grade Mathematics

What Is It We Expect Students to Learn?

Grade: Subject: Semester: Team Members:

Description of Standard	Example of Rigor	Prerequisite Skills	When Taught	Common Summative Assessment	Extension Standards
What is the essential standard to be learned? Describe in student-friendly vocabulary.	What does proficient student work look like? Provide an example and/or description.	What prior knowledge, skills, and/or vocabulary are needed for a student to master this standard?	When will this standard be taught?	What assessment(s) will be used to measure student mastery?	What will we do when students have already learned this standard?
I can compare whole numbers to 1,000 by using symbols <, =, >.	Example: What goes in the box to make this problem correct? 62 ☐ 21 + 31 < > = +	I know the place value of digits *from 1 to 1,000.* I understand key words: *greater than, less than, fewer, least, and most.*	September	CFAs designed by the second-grade team are administered halfway through and at the completion of the unit.	I can compare money written in decimal form.
I can use commutative and associative rules to simplify addition and check my answers.	Example: Which problem can you use to check your answer for 9 + 5 = 14? 13 − 5 = 9 14 − 9 = 5 5 + 9 = 14	I understand relationships within fact families.	October	Same as above	I can use commutative and associative rules to simplify multiplication and check my answers.

I can add and subtract multidigit numbers with regrouping.	I can follow steps when regrouping. I can count on and back. I can recognize when regrouping is necessary. I can add and subtract sums to 20 and differences from 20, and I relate addition and subtraction facts. Examples: $8 + 7 =$ $8 +$ what number $= 15$ Examples: a. $638 + 734 =$ b. Jose gathered 714 stickers and then gave 476 away to his friends. How many stickers does he have left? c. $+\,\dfrac{345}{465}$ $-\,\dfrac{387}{149}$	October–November	Same as above	I can solve multiplication and division problems. I can apply addition and subtraction skills to multistep problems involving multiple operations.
I can solve problems using combinations of coins and bills.	I know the value of bills and coins. I can add coins and bills together. I know symbols to use when writing money. 1¢ 25¢ 10¢ $1 $5 Example: What is the total value? $6.06 $6.36 $6.26	December	Same as above	I can create budgets for my classroom and determine how much money would be necessary to purchase supplies.

Source: © 2013 by Austin Buffum, Mike Mattos, and Chris Weber. Used with permission.

page 2 of 2

Tool: Identifying Important Questions to Study Together

Instructions: Brainstorm three to five research questions about topics that will prepare students to be successful in three areas: (1) long after they've left school (endurance), (2) classes that cross multiple academic domains (leverage), and (3) your content area at the next grade level (readiness; Reeves, 2002). Then use the reflection questions at the bottom of this template to identify an important question that your team can study together.

Endurance Questions	Leverage Questions	Readiness Questions
Sample: *How can we better help students engage in collaborative conversations where they build knowledge with one another?*	**Sample:** *How can we better help students use data as evidence to support claims?*	**Sample:** *How can we better help students understand the role that literary devices like foreshadowing and personification can play in written expression?*

Questions for Reflection

Which potential research questions do you think your learning team should prioritize? Why?

What patterns can you find in team-, school-, or district-level data to confirm that answering these questions together will help you achieve better results for the students that you serve?

Which questions are the most motivating to you as an individual? Why?

Additional Resources
What We Want Students to Learn

Reference

Reeves, D. B. (2002). *The leader's guide to standards: A blueprint for educational equity and excellence.* San Francisco: Jossey-Bass.

Protocol: Identifying Important Questions to Study Together

This protocol describes the process of using the endurance, leverage, and readiness test (Reeves, 2002) to brainstorm research questions that are worth studying.

1. **Introduction** (five minutes)

   A. A team member acting as facilitator introduces the purpose of the protocol: to help the learning team identify essential questions worth studying together in a cycle of collective inquiry.

   B. The facilitator introduces the three filters that teams should use when identifying questions worth studying together.

      i. **Endurance:** *Knowledge and skills that will prepare students to be successful long after they have left school*

      ii. **Leverage:** *Knowledge and skills that will prepare students to be successful in classes that cross academic domains*

      iii. **Readiness:** *Knowledge and skills that will prepare students to be successful in a specific content area at the next grade level*

2. **Brainstorming Questions** (fifteen minutes)

   A. Participants brainstorm questions that fall into each of the three filtering categories.

   B. The facilitator records the questions on a sheet of chart paper that can be easily viewed by all participants, polishing language and combining similar questions as they are offered.

   C. The goal is to generate three to five questions per filtering category.

3. **Prioritizing Questions** (ten minutes)

   A. Participants take turns identifying one or two questions that should be prioritized by the team.

   B. The facilitator asks probing questions to uncover the rationale from each participant.

      i. *"What patterns do we see in our team, school, or district data to confirm that answering this question together will help us achieve better results for the students we serve?"*

      ii. *"Why is this the right question for our learning team to study? What makes it important for preparing our students to be successful?"*

      iii. *"Would studying this question help us move our own priorities forward? Would it help us better implement school or district priorities?"*

4. **Voting** (five minutes)

   A. Using colored markers, highlighters, or stickers, individual participants indicate three questions that they would like to see the team study.

      i. *While it is likely that participants will select questions from more than one filtering category, it is not necessary.*

5. **Summarizing and Selecting Questions to Study** (fifteen minutes)

   A. The facilitator summarizes patterns in the questions selected by participants in step 4.

      i. *"The question that received the most votes was . . ."*

      ii. *"The question that received the least votes was . . ."*

      iii. *"There is lots of interest in studying . . ."*

      iv. *"There isn't any interest in studying . . ."*

page 1 of 2

B. The facilitator indicates connections between questions identified in step 4 and patterns in team, school, or district data sets and initiatives.

    i. *"Studying this question would make sense for this team because . . ."*

    ii. *"Students on our team could really benefit from a study of this question because . . ."*

    iii. *"Studying this question would help us move a school initiative forward."*

C. The facilitator proposes one or two questions that the team can begin studying together.

    i. *"Based on all this information, I think we should begin by studying _____ together."*

D. The facilitator asks participants to share their level of agreement with the questions selected for study on a scale from 0 to 5.

    i. *Zero represents complete disagreement. Five represents strong agreement.*

    ii. *If any participant gives a rating less than a 3, the facilitator asks for clarification.*

        a. "What concerns you about studying this question?"

        b. "Can you offer some revisions to the question that would make you more open to studying it?"

        c. "What alternative questions do you think we should prioritize? Why?"

E. Once consensus is reached, the facilitator shares the questions to be studied with both the team and the administration.

6. **Debriefing** (five minutes)

A. The facilitator leads a conversation on this question-setting experience.

    i. *"What did you like about our structured conversation? Why?"*

    ii. *"What would you change about our structured conversation? Why?"*

    iii. *"Do you think that the structure of this protocol helped or harmed our conversation? Why?"*

    iv. *"Do you think we achieved consensus during this structured conversation?"*

Reference

Reeves, D. B. (2002). *The leader's guide to standards: A blueprint for educational equity and excellence.* San Francisco: Jossey-Bass.

Tool: Spotting Patterns in Standardized Tests and Universal Screening Data

Instructions: Remember that school leaders, instructional coaches, special educators, or curriculum coordinators often have access to detailed information about the performance of your students and any learning gaps that need to be overcome. Ask one or more of those experts to answer each of the questions in the following template. Then, schedule a meeting with them to review the performance patterns that they spot in the data sets that they have access to.

Name of the professional who you will ask for information:		
Pattern Identified in Student Learning What performance patterns can you spot in the data sets available to you? Are there individual concepts that students are struggling with? Are there skills that they haven't mastered yet? What concepts have our students mastered already? What are their strengths as a group?	**Sources Used to Identify This Pattern** Does this pattern appear in standardized exam results? Does it also appear in universal screening results? Do we see similar results in common assessments given by learning teams here at school?	**Additional Notes** Is this a typical pattern in student performance or something unique to this group of students? Do different subgroups of students demonstrate different patterns of performance with this skill or concept? Which ones?

page 1 of 2

Questions for Team Reflection

After meeting with this professional or expert to learn more about the patterns of performance in your current student population, answer the following questions with your learning team.

- What does your team think about the gaps in learning identified by the school leader, instructional coach, special educator, or curriculum coordinator who you reached out to? Is there anything surprising in these findings, or were the gaps spotted ones that you expected to see?

- If you were to rank the gaps in learning identified by the school leader, instructional coach, special educator, or curriculum coordinator in order from "most urgent to address" to "least urgent to address," what would your list look like? Why?

- Are there any gaps that you think are missing from this list? What evidence do you have to support your hunch that these gaps are sources of concern for your students?

Tool: Helping Singletons Identify Academic Skills and Dispositions Worth Studying

Instructions: Use the six research-based lists of essential academic skills and dispositions and the following reflection questions to identify a collaborative focus for your learning team.

The Global Achievement Gap	Partnership for 21st Century Learning	College Readiness Skills
Students are adept at: • Thinking critically and solving problems • Collaborating across networks • Being agile and adaptable • Showing initiative and entrepreneurship • Displaying oral, written, and multimedia communication skills • Being curious and imaginative	Students are adept at: • Creativity and innovation • Critical thinking and problem solving • Communication and collaboration • Flexibility and adaptability • Initiative and self-direction • Productivity and accountability • Leadership and responsibility • Information and media literacy	Students are adept at: • Analytical reading and discussion • Persuasive writing • Drawing inferences and conclusions from texts • Analyzing conflicting source documents • Supporting arguments with evidence • Solving complex problems with no obvious answer
Key Competencies for Lifelong Learning	**Making Thinking Visible**	**Career Readiness Skills**
Students are adept at: • Communicating in the mother tongue • Communicating in foreign languages • Achieving mathematical competence and basic competencies in science and technology • Achieving digital competence • Learning to learn • Achieving social and civic competencies • Displaying a sense of initiative and entrepreneurship • Displaying cultural awareness and expression	Students are adept at: • Observing closely and describing what's there • Building explanations and interpretations • Reasoning with evidence • Making connections • Considering different viewpoints and perspectives • Capturing the heart and forming conclusions • Wondering and asking questions • Uncovering complexity and going beyond the surface of things	Students are adept at: • Considering the academic, social, and economic impact of decisions • Employing valid and reliable research strategies • Working productively in teams while using cultural and global competence • Utilizing critical thinking to make sense of problems and persevere in solving them • Communicating clearly, effectively, and with reason • Demonstrating creativity and innovation
Sources: European Parliament & Council of the European Union, 2006; Partnership for 21st Century Learning, 2019; Ritchhart, Church, & Morrison, 2011; Wagner, 2008.		

Source: Buffum, A., & Mattos, M. (2020). RTI at Work plan book. *Bloomington, IN: Solution Tree Press.*

Additional Resources
What We Want Students to Learn

Questions for Reflection

What patterns can you find in the academic skills and behaviors recommended in each of the six research-based lists?

Can you think of other professional organizations that may have created lists of academic skills and behaviors that would be worth consulting in order to find an area of professional focus for your team?

Which academic skills and behaviors do you think are the most important for students to master?

Which academic skills and behaviors do you think are missing from these six lists?

Which academic skills and behaviors have been emphasized in your school, district, or state?

Which academic skills and behaviors would be easy to integrate into the work that you already do in your classrooms?

Which academic skill or behavior would you like to make the focus of your collaborative team's efforts for the next school year?

References

European Parliament & Council of the European Union. (2006, December 18). *Recommendations of the European Parliament and the Council on key competencies for lifelong learning.* Accessed at http://eur-lex.europa.eu/legal-content /EN/ALL/?uri=celex%3A32006H0962 on January 22, 2020.

Partnership for 21st Century Learning. (2019). *Framework for 21st century learning.* Accessed at http://static.battelleforkids .org/documents/p21/P21_Framework_Brief.pdf on January 22, 2020.

Ritchhart, R., Church, M., & Morrison, K. (2011). *Making thinking visible: How to promote engagement, understanding, and independence for all learners.* San Francisco: Jossey-Bass.

Wagner, T. (2008). *The global achievement gap: Why even our best schools don't teach the new survival skills our children need—and what we can do about it.* New York: Basic Books.

Tool: Helping Singletons Identify Essential Outcomes to Study

Instructions: Working with your learning team, use the questions in the left column to begin brainstorming a plan for a meaningful skill-based cycle of inquiry.

Name of Learning Team:	
Questions	**Team Response**
What are the three to five most important skills that play a role in student success in the classrooms of every member of your learning team? Brainstorm to come up with a list. Then, prioritize those skills in order from the most important to the least important.	
Which of these skills are directly connected to your school's mission and vision? Which are already playing an important part in your ongoing efforts to grow as a staff? Which are most important to the success of the students in your community?	
Are there any school- or district-based data to support your team's belief that the skills you have identified are important enough to spend time studying them together? (Remember, administrative teams can often provide teams with a detailed look at student learning data in your school.)	
How are these skills applied in each of your unique classrooms? What are the similarities and differences in the ways that students use these skills across your classrooms?	
What would a student who has mastered the skills that your team has identified be able to do? Would mastery look different depending on your unique fields, or would there be similarities among the performances of successful students regardless of your discipline?	
What steps would you take in your own classroom to support students who are struggling with the skills that your team has identified? Would intervention look different depending on your unique fields, or are there similarities in the steps you would take as a teacher, regardless of your discipline?	

Source: Adapted from Ferriter, W. M., Graham, P., & Wight, M. (2013). Making teamwork meaningful: Leading progress-driven collaboration in a PLC. *Bloomington, IN: Solution Tree Press.*

Survey: Does Your Team Have a Guaranteed and Viable Curriculum?

Instructions: Following are a series of statements that can help you determine whether your team has a guaranteed and viable curriculum. Work individually to circle the number on the spectrum that best represents the current work of your team for each statement. Then, share your individual results with the other members of your learning team. Use the reflection questions at the end of this template to determine next steps worth taking.

Teachers on teams **without** a guaranteed and viable curriculum would say:						Teachers on teams **with** a guaranteed and viable curriculum would say:
I'm not always sure what other teachers on our team are teaching, or how they sequence instruction in our units.	1	2	3	4	5	I'm confident that every teacher on our team addresses the same outcomes at roughly the same time in each of our units.
There's *no way* I can get through everything that I'm supposed to teach in each of our units.	1	2	3	4	5	I'm confident that I can get through everything I'm expected to teach in each of our units.
Our team tries to teach everything in the required standards for our content area and grade level.	1	2	3	4	5	Our team has narrowed our focus by working together to create lists of essential and nonessential outcomes (need to knows and nice to knows) for all our units.
Our team hasn't ever looked to see how well our assessments align with what we want our students to know and be able to do.	1	2	3	4	5	Our team has looked carefully at *all* our assessments to make sure they are aligned with what we want students to know and be able to do.
I'm not sure that our team's assessments are as rigorous as we'd like them to be.	1	2	3	4	5	We have used the revised Bloom's (1956) taxonomy or Webb's (1997) Depth of Knowledge matrix to make sure that questions on our team's assessments match the level of rigor in the learning targets we are measuring.
Our team has never worked together to clearly define what mastery looks like on subjective tasks or performance-based assignments.	1	2	3	4	5	Our team creates sets of exemplars together that we use to clarify our expectations for subjective tasks or performance-based assignments.

Questions for Reflection

What can you celebrate about the findings in your guaranteed and viable curriculum survey?
What positive steps has your learning team already taken to develop a guaranteed and viable curriculum and deliver it to your students?

Which finding in your guaranteed and viable curriculum survey bothers you the most? Which finding is causing the greatest difficulties in your work as a teacher? As a member of a collaborative team? Which is the greatest roadblock to successful learning for the students who your learning team serves?

What's a tangible next step that your team could take to tighten up your guaranteed and viable curriculum? Could you look through your curriculum and identify standards that are nonessential to success in your classes? Could you sit down and rank your essential learning outcomes from most important to least important? Could you develop pretests to determine the standards that most of your students have already mastered?

References

Bloom, B. S. (Ed.). (1956). *Taxonomy of educational objectives, handbook I: Cognitive domain*. New York: Longman.

Webb, N. L. (1997). *Research monograph number 6: Criteria for alignment of expectations and assessments in mathematics and science education*. Washington, DC: Council of Chief State School Officers.

Tool: Guaranteed and Viable Curriculum Reflection Questions

Instructions: To begin building awareness about the important role that a guaranteed and viable curriculum plays in a professional learning community, answer the following questions with your learning team in an upcoming meeting.

Questions	Your Response
Educator and academic literary critic E. D. Hirsch Jr. (1999) says that the notion that all students in a school have access to the same curriculum is a "gravely misleading myth" (p. 26). Do you think that's true of the students of the teachers on your learning team? Are all students in every class being exposed to the same essential learning outcomes no matter who their teacher is? How close are you to this simple yet essential first step toward creating a guaranteed and viable curriculum?	
Author and educator Heidi Hayes Jacobs (2001) describes district curriculum guides as "well intended but fundamentally fictional accounts" of what students are actually learning in schools (p. 20). Do you think this is true of the curriculum guides created by your state and county? Are they an accurate portrayal of what the students in your school, at your grade level, or in your discipline are learning? Why or why not?	
The results of a Robert J. Marzano (2003) research study determine that it would take twenty-three years to adequately cover all the K–12 standards set for students. Is that still true of the curriculum that we are asked to teach students today? Is there too much content to reasonably cover in one school year? What implications does this carry for your learning team? What steps will you have to take in order to ensure a viable curriculum?	

References

Hirsch, E. D., Jr. (1999). *The schools we need and why we don't have them.* New York: Anchor Books.

Jacobs, H. H. (2001). New trends in curriculum: An interview with Heidi Hayes Jacobs. *Independent School, 61*(1), 18–22.

Marzano, R. J. (2003). *What works in schools: Translating research into action.* Alexandria, VA: Association for Supervision and Curriculum Development.

The Big Book of Tools for Collaborative Teams in a PLC at Work © 2020 Solution Tree Press • SolutionTree.com

Visit **go.SolutionTree.com/PLCbooks/BBTCT** and enter the unique access code found on the book's inside front cover to access this reproducible.

3

How Will We Know
Students Are Learning?

Once a collaborative team has identified grade-level essentials that every student must master, members work together to answer the second critical question in a PLC at Work: *How will we know students are learning?* (DuFour et al., 2016). Answering this question requires teams to develop and deliver common assessments for every unit in their required curriculum. Developing and delivering common assessments means that all the students who are served by teachers working on the same learning team:

> will be assessed using the same instrument or process, at the same time, or within a very narrow window of time. If the assessment is a paper-and-pencil test, it will be the same paper-and-pencil test. If the assessment is performance based, the assessment will focus on the same performance and teachers will use the same criteria in judging the quality of student work. (DuFour et al., 2016, p. 134)

Some common assessments given by learning teams are summative—delivered at the end of a unit of instruction and designed to give students a chance to *prove* what they have learned. Other common assessments are formative—delivered at predetermined points throughout a unit of instruction and designed to *improve* learning by generating information that teachers can use to make adjustments to their instructional plans and that students can use to make adjustments to their learning efforts (DuFour et al., 2016; Popham, 2008). In PLCs at Work, common *formative* assessments serve four primary purposes (DuFour & DuFour, 2012).

1. To help teachers identify students who are struggling to master—or who are already proficient with—essential concepts and skills

2. To help students track their *own* progress toward mastering essential concepts and skills

3. To provide teachers with evidence of their *individual* pedagogical strengths and weaknesses

4. To provide teams with evidence of their *collective* pedagogical strengths and weaknesses

Does this make sense to you? Collaborative teams in a PLC at Work know that they must rely on something more than instinct to determine whether students are mastering essential outcomes. Instead, they use results from common formative assessments to track progress by both student and standard, making it possible to develop and deliver targeted intervention and extension opportunities, ensuring the highest levels of learning for all.

Collaborative teams also use common formative assessment results *to study instruction*. "The question that drives inquiry into effective teaching for collaborative teams," argues Robert Eaker, architect of the Professional Learning Communities at Work process, "is are the kids learning—skill by skill—and how do we know?" (personal communication, February 8, 2019). Sometimes, common formative assessments reveal gaps in the instructional skill set of individual teachers, encouraging them to seek out new strategies for teaching essential concepts from their peers. Other times, common formative assessments reveal gaps in the instructional skill set of the entire team, encouraging members to work together to research, refine, and revise their shared approach to teaching essential concepts to students (DuFour & DuFour, 2012). In both cases, common formative assessments become valuable tools for creating urgency and improving the pedagogical capacity of learning teams.

Perhaps most importantly, common formative assessments can provide teachers with tangible evidence that their shared efforts are having a positive impact on student learning—and that evidence means everything. In fact, John Hattie (n.d.) would be quick to remind us that *collective teacher efficacy*—the practice with the greatest potential to considerably accelerate student achievement—only develops when teams can document the impact that their shared efforts are having on learners. In defining collective teacher efficacy, Hattie (n.d.) argues:

> It isn't just growth mindset. It's not just rah-rah thinking; it's not just, "Oh—we can make a difference!" But it is that combined belief that it is [teachers who cause] learning. It is not the students. It's not the students from particular social backgrounds. It's not all the barriers out there. Because when you fundamentally believe that you can make the difference, and then you feed it with the evidence that you are, that is dramatically powerful.

In order to build the collective efficacy of a collaborative team, common formative assessments must provide teachers with *instructionally actionable data* (Bailey & Jakicic, 2012). That means all questions on a common formative assessment should be tied to specific essential learning targets and should test for the common misconceptions that students hold about the concepts they are studying. Tying questions to specific essential learning targets and testing for common misconceptions makes it possible for teachers to use item analyses to quickly identify outcomes that individual students are struggling to master (Bailey & Jakicic, 2012). Common formative assessments should also be short—think fewer than ten questions tied to no more than three or four learning targets—and given frequently. When assessments cover *less* content, teams are *more* likely to respond to the results that they collect (Bailey & Jakicic, 2012). Finally, common formative assessment results should always be organized in ways that provide teams with opportunities to reflect on the impact that their professional choices are having on student learning. Data sorted by individual teacher can help teams spot members who have identified instructional strategies that are working and should be amplified across an entire hallway—an essential step for creating conversations that are explicitly structured to improve the classroom practice of teachers.

And in order to build the efficacy of the learners in their classrooms, collaborative teams integrate regular opportunities for student self-assessment into their assessment plan and into their instruction.

Giving Students Tools to Self-Assess

For assessment experts Rick Stiggins and Jan Chappuis (2010), the most effective student self-assessment efforts give learners chances to keep records of—and to report out on—the progress they are making toward mastering essential outcomes. Keeping records of progress over the course of a cycle of instruction builds the confidence of learners, providing tangible evidence to all students that they are academically capable and competent (Stiggins & Chappuis, 2010). Reporting on progress—particularly to important adults like parents and teachers—serves as a powerful reminder to students that they are responsible for moving their own learning forward (Stiggins & Chappuis, 2010). By developing the self-assessment abilities of their students, teachers can increase the overall assessment capacity of their classrooms, ensuring that "dollops of feedback" are available to every student, every day (Hattie, 1992, p. 9).

To introduce student self-assessment into your classroom, consider creating simple progress-tracking templates that students can refer to over the course of a unit of instruction. Progress-tracking templates will look different depending on your students' grade level, but all should do the following.

- List all the essential outcomes covered during the unit in student-friendly language.

- Provide students with a chance to rate their own levels of mastery on each essential outcome.

- Allow students to see changes in their levels of mastery over time.

Progress-tracking templates can also include these components.

- "Doing" tasks that students can complete in order to demonstrate mastery of individual outcomes

- Spaces for students to record grades earned on classroom assignments and assessments that are tied to each essential outcome

- A list of vocabulary words covered during a unit of study

Progress-tracking cards are the best tool for incorporating student self-assessment into the primary grades. A progress-tracking card lists one essential outcome that students are expected to master during a unit, along with several explicit tasks that students can use as checkpoints to determine how close they are to meeting or exceeding grade-level expectations. Progress-tracking cards also include a visual cue for each progress checkpoint that reminds students that they are growing as learners (see figure 3.1).

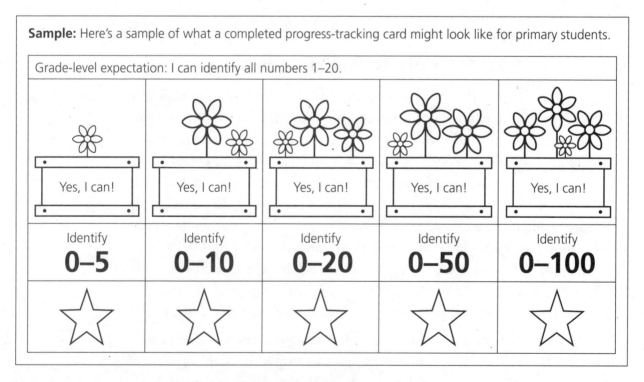

Sample: Here's a sample of what a completed progress-tracking card might look like for primary students.

Grade-level expectation: I can identify all numbers 1–20.				
Yes, I can!	Yes, I can!	Yes, I can!	Yes, I can!	Yes, I can!
Identify **0–5**	Identify **0–10**	Identify **0–20**	Identify **0–50**	Identify **0–100**
☆	☆	☆	☆	☆

Source: © 2017 by Mason Crest Elementary School. Adapted with permission.

Figure 3.1: Sample progress-tracking card for primary students.

Teachers using progress-tracking cards often create sets of three to five cards that are bound together with book rings for each student. Students then bring their card collections to learning stations and earn hole punches or stickers each time that they demonstrate mastery of a task listed at a progress checkpoint. Over time, card collections become tangible evidence that students can refer to as proof of their ability as learners and use in conferences with parents or teachers to report out on the progress that they are making toward meeting grade-level expectations.

Unit overview sheets are the best tool for incorporating student self-assessment into upper elementary, middle, and high school classrooms. A unit overview sheet lists three to five essential outcomes that students are expected to master during a unit, includes a list of essential vocabulary, and provides students with space to track their current levels of mastery and to record evidence that they have mastered individual concepts (see figure 3.2).

Learning teams should work together to create a unit overview sheet that students can use to track progress toward mastery during the next unit of study. In the Learning Target column, teams can list three to five essential outcomes for this unit

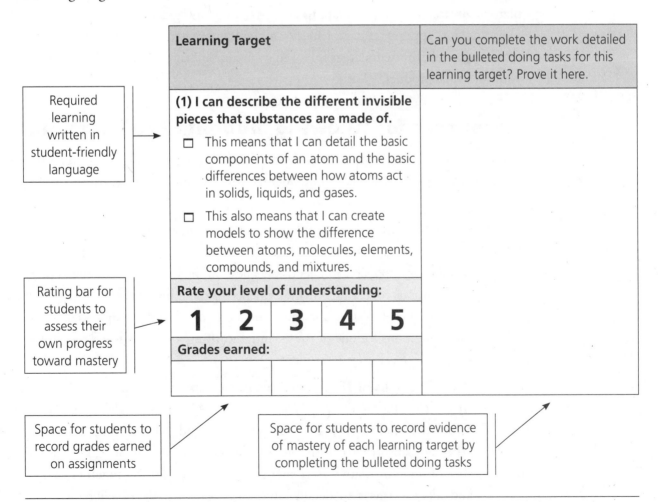

Figure 3.2: Sample unit overview sheet for upper elementary, middle, and high school students.

in student-friendly language. For each essential outcome, teams should include two or three bulleted *doing* tasks that students can complete to prove that they have mastered the outcome. Then, during classroom instruction, teachers give students time to rate their level of mastery of individual outcomes on a scale from 1 to 5, where 1 represents "This is new to me" and 5 represents "I have mastered this." Students can also record grades earned on classroom assignments to validate their self-ratings.

Over the course of a unit of study, students revisit their unit overview sheets during regular classroom activities, changing their ratings and adding new evidence to demonstrate mastery of important outcomes. Each check-in with a unit overview sheet helps students see places where they have made progress as learners and places where they still have progress to make. And like progress-tracking cards, unit overview sheets can be used by learners to report out on the progress that they are making toward mastering grade-level expectations during student-led conferences with parents or teachers.

Pages 130–137 include several tools for—and samples of—performance-tracking templates that can be used with students of all different grades and ability levels. A blank template that you can adapt to create your own progress-tracking card for primary students appears on page 130. For a blank template of a unit overview sheet, check page 132. This template is followed by a sample that can aid you in producing your own final product.

Resources for Knowing Students Are Learning

The resources in this chapter are all designed to help your learning team strengthen its assessment practices. The five fundamentals for assessing student learning include the following.

1. **"Tool: Building a Common Formative Assessment"** (page 102)—Common formative assessments are fundamental to the work of professional learning teams. It is impossible to relentlessly question the value of instructional practices without collecting reliable evidence of the impact that those practices are having on learners. Use this template to develop three potential assessment questions for one of the essential learning targets that your team has decided to teach to your students.

2. **"Tool: Using the ACID Test to Evaluate a Common Formative Assessment"** (pages 103–104)—In *Simplifying Common Assessment*, assessment experts Kim Bailey and Chris Jakicic (2017) recommend that teams use four basic criteria—which they call the ACID test—to evaluate the overall quality of the common formative assessments that they are writing together. Bailey and Jakicic's criteria are detailed in this template. Use them—along with the

reflection questions included at the end of this tool—to evaluate one of your upcoming formative assessments.

3. **"Tool: Performance Tracking Table"** (page 105)—One of the steps that teams can take to better assess the learning happening in their classrooms is to begin tracking observations of student performance during instruction. Observations are a valuable source of information that often goes overlooked by learning teams simply because they are difficult to collect and to document. To make that work easier, professors of education leadership Douglas Fisher and Nancy Frey (2012) recommend using simple tracking tables that detail the common errors that teachers expect students to make and include the initials of students making those errors. Here is a template that your learning team can use to turn individual observations into instructionally actionable data. Two sample versions follow on pages 106–108 to illustrate use of the performance tracking table.

4. **"Tools: Common Formative Assessment Data Trackers—Individual Results and Team Results"** (pages 109–113)—If teachers and learning teams are going to use common formative assessment results to improve classroom practice, they must create detailed data sets that sort results by individual teacher. Doing so can help teams identify teachers who are using strategies that produce meaningful learning gains for students. These two templates, one to track individual assessment results and one to collect data for the team as a whole, are designed to help both individual teachers and learning teams prepare their data for an upcoming conversation about a common formative assessment. These tools are followed on page 114 by a sample that is designed to help you see how they can be used.

5. **"Tool: Team Analysis of Common Formative Assessment Data"** (pages 116–117)—Collaborative teams use the evidence that they gather from common formative assessments both to inform their classroom practice and to intervene on behalf of students. While analyzing the results of your next common formative assessment, your learning team can use this template to make observations about your instruction and to plan remediation, additional practice, and extension opportunities for your students.

The additional resources for extending the assessment work of your team are as follows.

- **"Tool: Writing a Good Selected-Response Question"** (pages 119–120)—For many learning teams, *selected-response questions*, where the student chooses the correct response from a list of options, can be valuable tools for assessing learning because they are quick to write, deliver, and score. Better yet, if they are written deliberately, selected-response questions can provide teams with detailed information about the common misconceptions that are causing students to struggle with essential outcomes. Use this template to write an effective selected-response question for an upcoming assessment.

- **"Tool: Instructional Implications of Common Formative Assessment Data"** (pages 121–122)—Collaborative teams recognize that common formative assessments should help teachers evaluate the impact of their professional choices. When looking at your next data set, use this template to think through the instructional implications of the results that you have gathered.

- **"Tool: Individual Teacher Reflection on Student Learning Data"** (page 123)—If common formative assessments are going to have a positive impact on classroom practice, individual teachers need to reflect every time an assessment is given. Specifically, they need to examine student learning data, looking for places where they have pedagogical expertise to offer and places where they need to seek pedagogical support from their peers. Use this template to guide your reflection after your team's next common formative assessment. This tool is followed on page 124 by a sample designed to help you see how it can be used.

- **"Tools: Defining and Tracking Frequent Mistakes on a Common Formative Assessment"** (pages 125–129)—Assessment expert Chris Jakicic (2018) argues that common formative assessments only become powerful when learning teams deliberately track the kinds of mistakes that students are making on the assessments that the teachers give. By tracking common mistakes, teams can identify the misconceptions that are preventing students from mastering important outcomes and plan targeted interventions for students. Use these three templates to first define the mistakes that you expect to see frequently on your next common formative assessment and then compile, organize, and reflect on patterns in the data that you collect at the individual teacher and team levels.

- **"Tools: Student Self-Assessments"** (pages 130–137)—One of the highest-leverage instructional practices that teachers can incorporate into their classrooms is student self-assessment. By asking students to monitor their own progress toward mastering important outcomes, teachers shift responsibility for learning from the teacher to the student. Tracking progress toward mastery can also serve as a powerful confidence booster for students, who can see tangible evidence that they have mastered important outcomes. This book provides three different student self-assessment templates: (1) "Progress-Tracking Cards for Primary Students," (2) "Not Yet and You Bet Lists for Primary Students," and (3) "Unit Overview Sheets for Student

Self-Assessment in Upper Elementary, Middle, and High School." Use them to incorporate opportunities for student self-assessment into your classroom practices.

- **"Tool: Evidence of Practice in Action"** (pages 138–139)—On collaborative teams, data, not personal preferences, are used to evaluate the impact of every teaching strategy. Use this template to track the impact that the key instructional practices embraced by your learning team are having on student achievement and to identify a small set of high-leverage strategies that are worth using with regularity in your classroom.

- **"Tool: Evidence of Practice in Action—Teacher Self-Reflection"** (pages 140–141)—Once a learning team has used the "Evidence of Practice in Action" template (page 138) to identify a small set of key instructional practices that it plans to use with regularity, it is important for individual teachers to monitor their own ability with each of those strategies. Use this template to reflect on your work with one of your team's key instructional practices.

- **"Tool: Practice-Centered Peer Observation"** (pages 142–143)—Once collaborative teams have used common formative assessment data to identify a small handful of promising instructional strategies, they use peer observations to learn more about the impact that those strategies are having on students as learners. The key to ensuring that these peer observations feel safe and productive is to keep them focused on instructional practices, not people. Use this template to focus your next practice-centered peer observation.

- **"Tool: Understanding Common Assessment Strategies"** (page 144)—Before you can write effective assessments, it is important to think critically about the three main assessment strategies used in schools: (1) selected-response questions, (2) constructed-response questions, and (3) performance assessments (defined on page 144). Use this template to review and reflect on the strengths and weaknesses of each of these assessment strategies.

- **"Tool: Reflecting on the Dual Purposes of Common Formative Assessments"** (page 145)—Most teachers in a PLC at Work understand that common formative assessment data should be used to identify students in need of remediation, additional practice, or extension. Many forget, however, that common formative assessment data should also be used to improve the classroom practice of teachers on a learning team. Use this template, which highlights the thinking of author and education expert Kenneth C. Williams (2016), to introduce your team to the dual purposes of common formative assessments.

- **"Checklist: Rating Your Team's Common Formative Assessment Practices"** (page 146)—One of the reasons teams struggle to use common formative assessments effectively in a PLC at Work is that they don't always have a clear sense of the individual actions that teams have to take in order to turn assessments into useful tools for driving change for both teachers and students. Use this checklist to rate your team's current work with common formative assessments.

- **"Survey: Data Literacy"** (pages 147–148)—Because PLCs at Work focus on results and make every effort to ensure that all students are successful, effective manipulation of data is essential. This survey is intended to help teams learn more about their levels of data literacy. The results of this survey can be used by teams to identify specific behaviors that they need to develop in order to become experts at using data to improve both student learning and classroom practice.

Five Fundamental Resources

for Knowing Students Are Learning

Tool: Building a Common Formative Assessment

Instructions: This template is designed to help you write a short common formative assessment for one essential standard. Start by writing down the learning target you will assess and then checking one box in each column. Fill in your potential assessment questions, expected answers, and common mistakes. Three reminders about the characteristics of high-quality common formative assessments can be found at the bottom of this template.

Essential Learning Target to Be Assessed:

Depth of Knowledge Level of Target	Best Strategy for Assessing This Target	Percentage of Questions on District Benchmarks and Standardized Tests That Cover This Target	How Important This Target Is for Future Success in and Beyond School
☐ Recall and Reproduction ☐ Skills and Concepts ☐ Strategic Thinking ☐ Extended Thinking	☐ Selected response ☐ Constructed response ☐ Performance task ☐ Other:	☐ 0–5 percent ☐ 6–10 percent ☐ 11–15 percent ☐ More than 15 percent	☐ Not important ☐ Somewhat important ☐ Very important ☐ Essential

Potential Assessment Questions

Question	Expected Answer	Common Mistakes We Might See

Three Important Common Formative Assessment Reminders

1. A good common formative assessment will cover no more than three essential learning targets. Limiting the length of a common formative assessment makes it possible for teachers to analyze and then act on collected data in a timely manner.

2. A good common formative assessment should include at least three questions for each learning target that is being tested. That protects data sets against the impact of poorly written questions.

3. The complexity of a question should align with the complexity of the learning target it is designed to measure. That means performance tasks are unnecessary for lower-order learning targets that require recall and reproduction but essential for higher-order learning targets that require strategic or extended thinking.

Tool: Using the ACID Test to Evaluate a Common Formative Assessment

Instructions: Use the following questions to evaluate the overall quality of a common formative assessment written by your learning team.

A	Is the assessment **aligned** to the context, content, and rigor or complexity of the standards? Look at the language of the standard and the learning targets (from the unwrapped standard) in comparison to the task. Are the thinking types on the assessment aligned to those targets? Do the various items target the various levels of rigor or application (for example, Depth of Knowledge; Webb, 1997) represented in the learning targets? For example, is the difficulty of the task or questions at the same level as the target? Examine any exemplars related to your targeted level of complexity. Is the level of scaffolding or cueing appropriate? Is the designated level of mastery or proficiency appropriate and aligned?	**Your Response:**
C	Are the items on the assessment **clearly written**? Read the prompt and any distractors provided. By completing this task as written, will students be demonstrating the skills and concepts you are targeting? Will students understand what you want them to do?	**Your Response:**
I	Will this assessment be **informative** about student learning and produce meaningful data? Will teams benefit from gathering data on these learning targets in this fashion? Will specific information on learning targets steer teams toward meaningful interventions and support? Will this assessment be an opportunity to provide feedback to students?	**Your Response:**

page 1 of 2

D	Is the assessment **designed** to reflect and support the demands of the standards? Will the items ask students to show what they know in a way similar to high-stakes assessments? Are students asked to provide reasoning for their answers? Are students looking for evidence? Are students digging into information in a variety of texts and sources?	Your Response:

Questions for Reflection

What are the strengths of this assessment?

What are the weaknesses of this assessment?

What changes, if any, do you need to make to this assessment?

What strategies from this assessment can be easily integrated into future assessments?

Source: Adapted from Bailey, K., & Jakicic, C. (2017). Simplifying common assessment: A guide for Professional Learning Communities at Work. *Bloomington, IN: Solution Tree Press.*

Reference

Webb, N. L. (1997). *Research monograph number 6: Criteria for alignment of expectations and assessments in mathematics and science education.* Washington, DC: Council of Chief State School Officers.

Tool: Performance Tracking Table

Instructions: Work with your learning team to brainstorm a list of the common mistakes that students are likely to make in your upcoming unit of study; enter the items from that list in the **Errors We Expect to See** column. Then, every time that you assess student performance (*grading papers*, *looking at student work samples*, *making observations during class*, *listening to student reasoning during classroom conversations*, and so on), write the initials of students making common errors in the columns titled **Attempts 1** to **4**. Finally, use the reflection questions to help you determine how to move forward.

Task: _____

Errors We Expect to See	Attempt 1	Attempt 2	Attempt 3	Attempt 4

Questions for Reflection

What conclusions can you draw about next steps worth taking from the data that you have collected? Do similar patterns appear in the data of other members of your learning team?

What do these data suggest about your own instructional strengths and weaknesses? Are there specific subgroups of students that you are struggling or excelling with? Are there specific concepts that you are struggling or excelling at teaching? How do you know?

Which students need targeted remediation? Which students need extra practice? Which students need extension?

Sample 1: Performance Tracking Table—Elementary School Mathematics

Instructions: Work with your learning team to brainstorm a list of the common mistakes that students are likely to make in your upcoming unit of study; enter the items from that list in the **Errors We Expect to See** column. Then, every time that you assess student performance (*grading papers, looking at student work samples, making observations during class, listening to student reasoning during classroom conversations*, and so on), write the initials of students making common errors in the columns titled **Attempts 1** to **4**. Finally, use the reflection questions to help you determine how to move forward.

Task: Area Method of Multiplication for Fourth-Grade Students

Errors We Expect to See	Attempt 1	Attempt 2	Attempt 3	Attempt 4
Student adds too many zeros when multiplying multiples of ten.	XP, JM, SA, AK	XP, AK	AK	AK
Student does not line up place values correctly when adding partial products to find the solution.	XP, JM, HH, DL, AK, TD, IG, DD, MP, SP, DP	XP, JM, DL, AK, IG, DD, MP, SP	XP, AK, MP, IG, SP	AK, IG
Student does not expand numbers correctly when recording the hundreds, tens, and ones.	MP, SP, DP	DP		
Student makes a multiplication fact error.	DMT, DD, XP	DMT, DD, XP	DMT, DD, XP	DMT, DD

Questions for Reflection

What conclusions can you draw about next steps worth taking from the data that you have collected? Do similar patterns appear in the data of other members of your learning team?

I am optimistic about these results. Here's why: the most common error—lining up place values correctly when adding partial products—is not fundamentally connected to the mathematics involved in using the area method of multiplication to solve problems. Instead, in most cases, it is a simple factor of not being careful when writing out problems. I notice many of the students in this list are also still developing gross and fine motor skills. Their handwriting, not their mathematical understanding, could be causing the problems that I am seeing. My solution will be to give these students large-grid graph paper and encourage them to write individual numbers into individual boxes on the graph paper. My prediction is that this will help students line up place values correctly.

The Big Book of Tools for Collaborative Teams in a PLC at Work © 2020 Solution Tree Press • SolutionTree.com
Visit **go.SolutionTree.com/PLCbooks/BBTCT** and enter the unique access code found on the book's inside front cover to access this reproducible.

Five Fundamental Resources
Knowing Students Are Learning

What do these data suggest about your own instructional strengths and weaknesses? Are there specific subgroups of students that you are struggling or excelling with? Are there specific concepts that you are struggling or excelling at teaching? How do you know?

Something that I'm doing to teach students to expand their place value numbers when setting up their initial grids is working well. That's interesting to me largely because my students are still struggling to line up their place values when adding partial sums. It is surprising that they can do one task but not the other. The pattern that I notice the most, though, is that the students who repeat mistakes time and again in all these areas are students who came to my class behind by a grade level or two in mathematics. This fits a pattern for me: my strategies generally work for students who are on grade level to begin with, but I struggle with students who have gaps in prerequisite knowledge. I need to find someone on my team who is good at teaching grade-level concepts to students who are behind and ask him or her for ideas.

Which students need targeted remediation? Which students need extra practice? Which students need extension?

I need to meet with Anya, Diego, Xavion, and Jared sometime during our intervention time to give them some additional reteaching. They continue to appear repeatedly in my observations. I am going to put together a few additional practice activities for the rest of my students as an initial intervention to see if that works.

Source: Adapted from Fisher, D., & Frey, N. (2012). Making time for feedback. Educational Leadership, 70*(1), 42–46.*

Common errors adapted from The Tarheelstate Teacher. (2015, December 6). Multiplying with the area model error analysis *[Blog post]. Accessed at https://tarheelstateteacher.com/blog/multiplying-with-the-area-model-error-analysis on August 5, 2019.*

Sample 2: Performance Tracking Table—Middle School Science

Instructions: Work with your learning team to brainstorm a list of the common mistakes that students are likely to make in your upcoming unit of study; enter the items from that list in the **Errors We Expect to See** column. Then, every time that you assess student performance (*grading papers*, *looking at student work samples*, *making observations during class*, *listening to student reasoning during classroom conversations*, and so on), write the initials of students making common errors in the columns titled **Attempts 1** to **4**. Finally, use the reflection questions to help you determine how to move forward.

Task: Lab Report for a Sixth-Grade Science Student

Errors We Expect to See	Attempt 1	Attempt 2	Attempt 3	Attempt 4
Hypothesis includes more than one testable variable.	MR, LR, HS, GT, JT	MR, LR, HS	HS	
Procedures are missing critical steps and could not be accurately followed by another scientist.	MR, LR, HS, GT, JT, JE, DD, NE	MR		
Graph or table fails to effectively communicate findings (sloppy, inaccurate information is included; unit labels are missing; scale on *y*-axis is laid out incorrectly).	DQT			
Conclusion doesn't include specific references to data collected in lab.	MR, LR, HS, SC, JL, KP, AA, DC, SS, KA, EW, JZ, NP, KR, JS	MR, LR, HS, SC, JL, KP, AA, DC, KA, JZ, NP, KR, JS, XP	MR, LR, HS, SC, JL, KP, DC, KA, JZ, NP, KR, JS, XP	MR, LR, HS, SC, JL, KP, DC, KA, JZ, NP, KR, JS, XP

Questions for Reflection

What conclusions can you draw about next steps worth taking from the data that you have collected? Do similar patterns appear in the data of other members of your learning team?

One of the things that we noticed across all our performance tracking templates is that we are all struggling to teach students to write proper conclusions for their labs. They don't see the connection between the data that we are collecting in the lab and the conclusions that they are drawing as scientists. One of the things that we can do to help with that is to continue to focus on our "Claim-Evidence-Reasoning" tasks in class. If we do those frequently, students should start to see that all claims need to be backed up with evidence, and that in a lab, collected data are the best evidence for supporting conclusions.

What do these data suggest about your own instructional strengths and weaknesses? Are there specific subgroups of students that you are struggling or excelling with? Are there specific concepts that you are struggling or excelling at teaching? How do you know?

Something that I'm doing to teach students to create graphs is really working. All my students, regardless of class, are making good graphs. I think it might be because we do a bunch of "body graphs" at the beginning of the year. That strategy is always engaging to the students, and I think that it helps them remember components of a good graph when they are asked to make one later.

Which students need targeted remediation? Which students need extra practice? Which students need extension?

I've got a whole handful of students who need help integrating data into their conclusion paragraphs. Henry also needs help with hypotheses. I can deliver that intervention during our next schoolwide intervention period.

Source: Adapted from Fisher, D., & Frey, N. (2012). Making time for feedback. Educational Leadership, 70*(1), 42–46.*

Tool: Common Formative Assessment
Data Tracker—Individual Results

Instructions: After filling in your name and the name of the assessment that you are giving, record the essential outcomes you are covering; if this assessment tests multiple outcomes, include the questions that are designed to measure each outcome. Then, while scoring student papers, indicate correct (•) and incorrect (X) answers to each question. Finally, use the reflection questions at the end of the table to help you prepare for an upcoming team conversation about the results of this common formative assessment.

Name of Teacher:
Name of Assessment:
Essential Outcomes Covered by Assessment:

Questions Answered Correctly and Incorrectly

(Use a • for correct answers and an **X** for incorrect answers.)

Name of Student	1	2	3	4	5	6	7	8	9	10	Teacher Reflection

Name of Student	1	2	3	4	5	6	7	8	9	10	Teacher Reflection

The Big Book of Tools for Collaborative Teams in a PLC at Work © 2020 Solution Tree Press • SolutionTree.com
Visit **go.SolutionTree.com/PLCbooks/BBTCT** and enter the unique access code found on the book's inside front cover to access this reproducible.

Questions for Individual Reflection

What patterns can you spot in the data from this common formative assessment? Are there individual questions that high percentages of your students answered correctly? Are there individual questions that high percentages of your students answered incorrectly? Have certain subgroups of students succeeded or struggled on this common formative assessment?

Are any of the patterns that you spotted in your common formative assessment data surprising to you? Did your students do better than you expected on any individual questions? Worse than you expected? Why are those patterns surprising?

What do these patterns mean for you as an instructor? Are there concepts and student subgroups that you excel at teaching? Are there concepts and student subgroups that you are struggling to teach? What will your next steps be?

Tool: Common Formative Assessment
Data Tracker—Team Results

Instructions: After filling in the name of the assessment your team is giving, record the essential outcomes you are covering; if the assessment tests multiple outcomes, include the questions that are designed to measure each outcome. Include each team member's name in the left column, then indicate the percentage of students who answered each question correctly. Finally, use the team reflection questions to help you determine how to move forward.

Five Fundamental Resources
Knowing Students Are Learning

Name of Assessment:										
Essential Outcomes Covered by Assessment:										

Percentage of Students Who Correctly Answered Each Question on This Assessment

Teacher	Question Number									
	1	**2**	**3**	**4**	**5**	**6**	**7**	**8**	**9**	**10**
Sample: Mr. Nowak	78	93	56	87	89	89	97	82	68	90
Overall Team Averages:										

The Big Book of Tools for Collaborative Teams in a PLC at Work © 2020 Solution Tree Press • SolutionTree.com
Visit **go.SolutionTree.com/PLCbooks/BBTCT** and enter the unique access code found on the book's inside front cover to access this reproducible.

Questions for Team Reflection

Are there individual teachers who have identified instructional practices that are particularly effective at teaching the concepts and skills covered on this assessment? What strategies are they using in their classrooms? Would those same strategies work in other classrooms? Can you use those strategies when teaching different concepts and skills to students?

Are there any concepts and skills that your entire team is struggling to teach well? Why is that? What makes those concepts and skills so challenging for students to master? What strategies are you using to teach those concepts and skills? Where can you find new ideas for teaching those concepts and skills to students?

What do these patterns mean for you as a team of instructors? Can these patterns help you plan more effective intervention or extension experiences for students? Can these patterns help you pinpoint an area for continued study for your learning team? What next steps will you take to address those patterns?

Five Fundamental Resources
Knowing Students Are Learning

page 2 of 2

Sample: Common Formative Assessment
Data Tracker—Team Results

Instructions: After filling in the name of the assessment your team is giving, record the essential outcomes you are covering; if the assessment tests multiple outcomes, include the questions that are designed to measure each outcome. Include each team member's name in the left column, then indicate the percentage of students who answered each question correctly. Finally, use the team reflection questions to help you determine how to move forward.

Name of Assessment: Fourth Grade—Comparing Multidigit Whole Numbers

Essential Outcomes Covered by Assessment:

This assessment covered one essential outcome: I can read and write multidigit whole numbers using base-ten numerals, number names, and expanded form. I can also accurately compare two multidigit numbers based on meanings of the digits in each place, using the >, =, and < symbols.

Percentage of Students Who Correctly Answered Each Question on This Assessment

Teacher	Question Number									
	1	**2**	**3**	**4**	**5**	**6**	**7**	**8**	**9**	**10**
Mr. Nowak	78	93	56	87	89	89	97	82	68	90
Ms. Morosini	83	90	83	85	91	74	95	83	63	91
Mrs. Messenger	79	91	51	87	88	92	94	85	71	90
Mrs. Chuddy	81	92	63	88	91	90	97	85	65	93
Overall Team Averages:	80	92	63	87	90	86	96	84	67	91

Questions for Team Reflection

Are there individual teachers who have identified instructional practices that are particularly effective at teaching the concepts and skills covered on this assessment?

Question 3 covered the differences between numbers written in base-ten numerals and expanded form. Ms. Morosini used an activity where students compared the different place values in money to the different place values in multidigit numbers. Specifically, she showed students how different place values in money were worth different numbers of pennies. For example, she had students work with values like $1.83, making a pile of 100 pennies, 80 pennies, and 3 pennies. That seems to have reinforced the base-ten idea of the expanded form of the numerals. Ms. Morosini also saw higher levels of motivation simply because students were working with money!

Are there any concepts and skills that your entire team is struggling to teach well?

Question 9 asked students to determine if 2,100 is greater or less than 2,090. We aren't certain why so many of our students got this wrong. Our guess is that because the numbers are obviously close to one another, the presence of a 9 made students think that 2,090 was the bigger number. What's interesting is that students didn't have trouble with questions that asked for comparisons between three- and four-digit numbers. (Question 8, for example, asked for a greater- and less-than comparison between 1,385 and 678.) The only time that we see high rates of mistakes is comparing numbers with the same number of digits, and competing digits that are close to one another.

What do these patterns mean for you as a team of instructors?

First, we should plan some intervention around questions 3 and 9. Ms. Morosini is going to bring the worksheet that she uses with her pennies activity to our next team meeting so we can see how she uses it. We might also want to consider taking questions 5 and 7 off our common assessment. Both ask students to identify the base-ten numerals for numbers that are written with number names. It's clear that students don't struggle with that—so we could replace the questions with something more meaningful.

Five Fundamental Resources
Knowing Students Are Learning

Tool: Team Analysis of Common Formative Assessment Data

Subject of Common Formative Assessment: _____

Step 1: Reflecting on Your Data

Instructions: Working with your learning team, look back at your data set for this common formative assessment and draw three conclusions together. To draw an effective conclusion, start by making an observation about a pattern that you see in your data set. Then, record a reaction to that observation. Finally, develop a plan of action to address the pattern that you see in your observation.

Our Observations	Our Reactions	Our Next Actions
What patterns catch your attention in the data you have collected? Which essential outcomes are students struggling with? Are certain questions missed frequently? Are certain subgroups of students missing questions frequently? Have certain teachers discovered instructional practices that are working?	*What do you think these patterns mean? Are certain questions written poorly? Is there a process or practice that students are struggling with? Are there vocabulary words that may have confused students? Is it possible that students have yet to master core skills and concepts that are essential for answering these questions?*	*What will your learning team do next to address this trend or pattern in the data that you've collected? Will you reteach a basic skill? Rewrite a question? Reassess a concept? Provide remediation or enrichment for a group of students? Revisit the way that you are teaching a skill or concept?*

Step 2: Developing an Intervention Plan Based on Your Data

Instructions: Determine how you will provide additional time and support, extra practice, or extension opportunities to your students.

	Students in Need of Extra Support *Organize your lists by teacher to make it easier to plan your next steps.*	Planned Instructional Strategy *What extra instruction will you offer to these students? Who will plan these learning experiences? Who will deliver them? When will these interventions happen?*
Additional Time and Support List the students in your classes who you think need direct reteaching because they are making significant conceptual mistakes when answering questions on your common formative assessment.		
Extra Practice List the students who you think have mastered the concept covered on this assessment, but who are making simple mistakes that can be corrected with additional practice instead of direct reteaching.		
Extensions List the students who you know have mastered the concept covered on this assessment and are ready to move beyond grade-level expectations.		

Source: Adapted from Bailey, K., & Jakicic, C. (2012). Common formative assessment: A toolkit for Professional Learning Communities at Work. Bloomington, IN: Solution Tree Press.

Five Fundamental Resources
Knowing Students Are Learning

Additional Resources

for Knowing Students Are Learning

Tool: Writing a Good Selected-Response Question

Step 1: Defining Common Mistakes

Instructions: Define three common mistakes or misunderstandings students have when working with this content.

Common Mistake or Misunderstanding 1	Common Mistake or Misunderstanding 2	Common Mistake or Misunderstanding 3

Step 2: Writing the Question

Instructions: Write your selected-response question, then use the prompts to come up with unique distractors that are tied to the common mistakes or misunderstandings you identified in step 1. Finally, use the reflection questions to reflect on the reliability of the question and distractors that you have written.

Question:	
Answer Choices	
Correct answer:	
Answer students would give if they were making common mistake 1:	
Answer students would give if they were making common mistake 2:	
Answer students would give if they were making common mistake 3:	

page 1 of 2

Questions for Reflection

To ensure that your question and distractors are reliable, ask yourself the following questions, drawn from the work of assessment experts Kim Bailey and Chris Jakicic (2019).

- Is your question written as a complete sentence?

- Are all your answer choices reasonable so that students can't easily eliminate an obviously wrong choice?

- Are all your answer choices similar lengths with parallel grammar so that students can't make predictions about correct answers by spotting patterns in the structure of your writing?

- Is your correct answer the only correct answer—or could students make a case for more than one right answer from your list of distractors?

Reference

Bailey, K., & Jakicic, C. (2019). *Make it happen: Coaching with the four critical questions of PLCs at Work*. Bloomington, IN: Solution Tree Press.

Tool: Instructional Implications of Common Formative Assessment Data

Step 1: Detail the Practices Used to Prepare Students for This Common Formative Assessment

Instructions: Use the following questions to help you think through the strategies that you are using to teach essential learning targets to your students.

Questions	Your Response
Which essential learning targets were you trying to teach on this assessment?	
How did you teach these essential learning targets? *Did you use group activities? Tiered lessons? Digital tools for reviewing content? Worksheets developed by team members? Lessons that integrated technology or hands-on tasks?*	
What are our general perceptions about the strategies that we used to teach these essential learning targets? *Were they easy to implement? Did they work well with all groups of students? Are we confident that they helped all students master the essential learning targets on this assessment? What didn't work well?*	

Step 2: Look for Patterns in Your Data Set

Instructions: Compile a list of three to five patterns that you can spot in your common formative assessment data. Remember that you will be using these patterns to reflect on the overall impact that your professional choices are having on your students as learners. Also, remember that the patterns you select to guide your choices should be objective facts rather than opinions or judgments.

Additional Resources
Knowing Students Are Learning

page 1 of 2

Examples	Your Response
• *Almost 80 percent of our students missed question 4.* • *The students on our team who speak another language all struggled with questions that required working through multiple steps.* • *Our students can answer basic recall questions, but they are struggling to apply those basic facts in the context of broader questions.* • *Most of our students are showing higher levels of mastery now than they did on our pretest.*	

Step 3: Draw Conclusions About Your Instructional Practices

Instructions: Using the patterns you identified in step 2, draw some initial conclusions about the overall value of the instructional practices that you are using to teach the essential learning targets covered on this common formative assessment.

Prompts	Your Response
The pattern that surprised us the most in today's data set was:	
The data that we have collected from this common formative assessment have left us convinced that:	
The data that we have collected from this common formative assessment have us wondering:	
Our next action will be:	

The Big Book of Tools for Collaborative Teams in a PLC at Work © 2020 Solution Tree Press • SolutionTree.com
Visit **go.SolutionTree.com/PLCbooks/BBTCT** and enter the unique access code found on the book's inside front cover to access this reproducible.

Tool: Individual Teacher Reflection on Student Learning Data

Instructions: Use this template to reflect on where you can offer your pedagogical expertise and where you might need pedagogical support from your peers after your team's next common formative assessment.

Questions to Consider	Your Response
What is an area where your team's students *excelled* on your recent common assessment?	
What is an area where your team's students *struggled* on your recent common assessment?	
What concepts or skills on your recent common assessment *are you particularly effective at teaching*? How do you teach those concepts or skills to students? What is unique about your practice? Who can you *lend your expertise* to on your learning team? What kind of support can you offer? When will you reach out?	
What concepts or skills on your recent common assessment *do you struggle to teach*? Why do you think you struggle with these concepts or skills? Do you think you need a new tool or strategy to try, or do you think you need deeper support in order to teach these concepts and skills better? Who can you reach out to for help? What kind of support will you ask for? When will you reach out?	

Additional Resources
Knowing Students Are Learning

Sample: Individual Teacher Reflection on Student Learning Data

Individual reflection about my own practice as a classroom teacher is my favorite part of the PLC process. I'm drawing on my own personal and professional experience in creating this sample reflection, based on a performance tracking task that my team and I completed to measure the progress our students were making toward mastering scientific method lab skills. My data set for that performance tracking task can be found on page 108.

Instructions: Use this template to reflect on where you can offer your pedagogical expertise and where you might need pedagogical support from your peers after your team's next common formative assessment.

Questions to Consider	Your Response
What is an area where *your team's students* excelled on your recent common assessment?	Looking at all the performance tracking tables from our team, it's easy to see that making graphs is a skill that our students don't really struggle with. Given that we haven't done a lot of direct instruction on graphing, I'm guessing that means our students learned a lot about graphs either in previous grades or in mathematics class. If that's true, we can probably scale back on our graphing lessons to save instructional time.
What is an area where *your team's students* struggled on your recent common assessment?	Looking back at all the performance tracking tables from our team, it's also easy to see that our students don't really understand how to incorporate data into their conclusions. It seems like they see those two parts of the lab report as completely separate. It's almost like they don't realize that their data should inform their conclusions, and that their work as authors of a lab report is to make those connections explicit.
What concepts or skills on your recent common assessment *are you particularly effective at teaching*? How do you teach those concepts or skills to students? What is unique about your practice? Who can you *lend your expertise* to on your learning team? What kind of support can you offer? When will you reach out?	I noticed that my students did really well compared to the students in other classrooms on writing procedures. I wonder if that's because I had my students swap procedures with other lab groups, conduct the lab exactly as described, and then provide feedback to one another. That took a lot of time, but it seems to have sent the message that scientists have to carefully craft their procedures so that *others* can follow them as written. Maybe the time was worth it. And maybe that's an idea I can share with Tom. He mentioned that his students struggled with procedures during our data review meeting. I think I'll reach out to him during planning this week and talk him through the process that I used. It's something easy and fun that he could incorporate into his class.
What concepts or skills on your recent common assessment *do you struggle to teach*? Why do you think you struggle with these concepts or skills? Do you think you need a new tool or strategy to try, or do you think you need deeper support in order to teach these concepts and skills better? Who can you reach out to for help? What kind of support will you ask for? When will you reach out?	What I noticed is that I am struggling to get results from my in-class resource (ICR) students. I guess that doesn't totally surprise me—I always feel more confident in my academically gifted (AG) classes. When I ask questions in my AG classes, I can see light bulbs going off in the minds of those students, but when I ask those same questions in my ICR classes, I get a lot of blank stares. I think what I need in order to improve my teaching is some help with writing a sequence of questions that can move my ICR students to the same conclusions that my AG students are making with just one or two higher-order questions. I know that Joyce is good at differentiating for special needs students. I'm going to ask her how she does this work with her ICR class sometime during planning this week.

Tool: Defining Frequent Mistakes on a Common Formative Assessment

Instructions: Together with your learning team, brainstorm a list of three frequent mistakes that students are likely to make on your upcoming common formative assessment. Then fill in the corresponding conceptual misunderstandings and potential questions to test for them. Finally, use the reflection questions to help you determine how to move forward.

Concept Covered on This Common Formative Assessment: _____

Mistake Students Are Likely to Make About the Content on This Common Formative Assessment	Conceptual Misunderstanding That This Common Mistake Represents	Potential Questions for Our Common Formative Assessment to Test for This Conceptual Misunderstanding

The Big Book of Tools for Collaborative Teams in a PLC at Work © 2020 Solution Tree Press • SolutionTree.com
Visit **go.SolutionTree.com/PLCbooks** to download this free reproducible.

Questions for Reflection

Do you have questions that are specifically designed to elicit information about each of the mistakes or misconceptions that your team expects to see on this common formative assessment? Which questions are you the most confident will provide useful information about students' misunderstandings? Which questions are you the least confident about? Why?

What other barriers—challenging vocabulary, question structure, student experience—could keep students from answering these potential questions correctly? How will you address those barriers?

Which mistake do you think students will make the most often on your upcoming common formative assessment? Why?

Tool: Tracking Frequent Mistakes on a Common Formative Assessment—Individual Teacher

Instructions: Once your learning team has used the "Defining Frequent Mistakes on a Common Formative Assessment" template (page 125) to identify three mistakes that students are likely to make on an upcoming common formative assessment, use this template to keep track of *the actual mistakes the students in your classroom make*. Doing so will give you feedback about the strengths and weaknesses of your instructional practices and help you target individual students for specific interventions.

Name of Common Formative Assessment: _____

Teacher Name:				
Student Name	**Common Mistakes Made** (Circle all that apply.)			**Likely Intervention Needed** (Check one.)
	Mistake 1	Mistake 2	Mistake 3	☐ Additional practice ☐ Quick review ☐ Extensive reteaching
	Mistake 1	Mistake 2	Mistake 3	☐ Additional practice ☐ Quick review ☐ Extensive reteaching
	Mistake 1	Mistake 2	Mistake 3	☐ Additional practice ☐ Quick review ☐ Extensive reteaching
	Mistake 1	Mistake 2	Mistake 3	☐ Additional practice ☐ Quick review ☐ Extensive reteaching
	Mistake 1	Mistake 2	Mistake 3	☐ Additional practice ☐ Quick review ☐ Extensive reteaching
	Mistake 1	Mistake 2	Mistake 3	☐ Additional practice ☐ Quick review ☐ Extensive reteaching
	Mistake 1	Mistake 2	Mistake 3	☐ Additional practice ☐ Quick review ☐ Extensive reteaching
	Mistake 1	Mistake 2	Mistake 3	☐ Additional practice ☐ Quick review ☐ Extensive reteaching

page 1 of 2

Student Name	Common Mistakes Made (Circle all that apply.)			Likely Intervention Needed (Check one.)
	Mistake 1	Mistake 2	Mistake 3	☐ Additional practice ☐ Quick review ☐ Extensive reteaching
	Mistake 1	Mistake 2	Mistake 3	☐ Additional practice ☐ Quick review ☐ Extensive reteaching
	Mistake 1	Mistake 2	Mistake 3	☐ Additional practice ☐ Quick review ☐ Extensive reteaching
Class Totals How many students in your class made each of the common mistakes that your learning team expected to see on this assessment?				

Questions for Reflection

What patterns can you spot in the kinds of mistakes that your students made on this common formative assessment?

How do these patterns compare to the patterns that peers on your learning team observed in their students' work? Are students making similar mistakes across your entire team?

Did large numbers of students make mistakes that your team didn't already anticipate? If so, what were those mistakes? Did your peers see students making those same unanticipated mistakes?

Do you have a high level of confidence in the instructional practices that you used to teach this concept to your students? Why or why not?

Who can you get support from when planning your next steps? Who will you support?

The Big Book of Tools for Collaborative Teams in a PLC at Work © 2020 Solution Tree Press • SolutionTree.com
Visit **go.SolutionTree.com/PLCbooks/BBTCT** and enter the unique access code found on the book's inside front cover to access this reproducible.

Tool: Tracking Frequent Mistakes on a Common Formative Assessment—Team Results

Instructions: Once your learning team has used the "Defining Frequent Mistakes on a Common Formative Assessment" template (page 125) to identify three mistakes that students are likely to make on an upcoming common formative assessment and individual teachers have used the "Tracking Frequent Mistakes on a Common Formative Assessment—Individual Teacher" template (page 127) to spot patterns in their own classrooms, record, by team member, the total number of students making each of the frequent mistakes on your recent common formative assessment. Then, add them up to reach a total number of students on your team who made each mistake. Finally, use the reflection questions to help you determine how to move forward.

Concept Covered on This Common Formative Assessment: _____

Teacher Name	Mistake 1	Mistake 2	Mistake 3
Team Totals			

Questions for Reflection

What patterns can you spot in the kinds of mistakes that the students of your learning team made on this common formative assessment? What can you learn about your students and your instructional practices from those patterns?

Did some members of your learning team have more success teaching this concept than others? What unique strategies did they use to achieve those results?

What steps will you take to intervene for students who are still struggling? Has your team identified or developed additional practice tasks yet? How about quick review activities? Can you group students across classrooms to provide extensive reteaching? When will this work get completed?

Tool: Progress-Tracking Cards for Primary Students

At Mason Crest Elementary School in Northern Virginia, primary students receive a ring-bound booklet that includes individual progress-tracking cards detailing levels of mastery for each essential outcome covered during a unit of study. As students work to master each essential outcome, they use a star-shaped hole punch to record their current level of performance. By the end of each unit, students can flip through their progress-tracking cards to identify outcomes that they have mastered and outcomes that they are still working to master. Visit https://twitter .com/fcpsr3/status/925397646684184577 to view an example of a progress-tracking card collection on a book ring that Fairfax County Public Schools Region 3 tweeted to laud the Mason Crest kindergartners' goal setting.

You can use the following template to create your own progress-tracking cards.

Visit http://bit.ly/primaryprogresstracking for an editable digital copy of this template.

Progress-Tracking Card Template

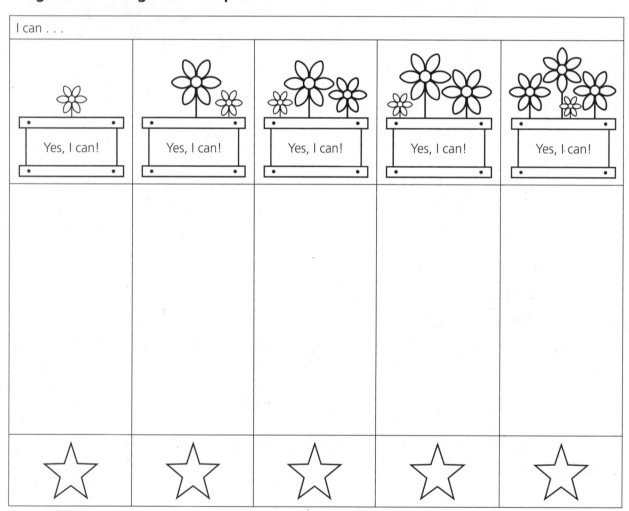

Source: © 2017 by Mason Crest Elementary School. Adapted with permission.

Tool: Not Yet and You Bet Lists for Primary Students

Instructions: Work with your teachers to identify three or four things that you are currently working to master. Write those things in pencil in the **Not Yet List** column of the following table. Each time that you master something in your **Not Yet List**, erase it and then move it to the **You Bet List** column of your table. That's proof that you are a learner!

Not Yet List *Content and skills that I am still working to master*	You Bet List *Content and skills that I have mastered*

Questions for Reflection

Which items on your You Bet list are you the proudest of mastering? Why?

Which items on your Not Yet list are you the closest to mastering? What steps could you take to move even closer to mastering those items?

List some of the strategies that you used to master the items on your You Bet list. Do you see any patterns in the strategies that typically help you master new content and skills? Can you apply any of those strategies to mastering the items in your Not Yet list?

Tool: Unit Overview Sheet for Student Self-Assessment in Upper Elementary, Middle, and High School

Name:
Unit:

Essential Questions

☐	☐	☐
☐	☐	☐

Learning Target	Can you complete the work detailed in the bulleted doing tasks for this learning target? Prove it here.

Rate Your Current Level of Understanding

1	2	3	4	5

Grades Earned on Assignments and Assessments

Learning Target	Can you complete the work detailed in the bulleted doing tasks for this learning target? Prove it here.

Rate Your Current Level of Understanding				
1	**2**	**3**	**4**	**5**

Grades Earned on Assignments and Assessments

Learning Target	Can you complete the work detailed in the bulleted doing tasks for this learning target? Prove it here.

Rate Your Current Level of Understanding				
1	**2**	**3**	**4**	**5**

Grades Earned on Assignments and Assessments

Learning Target	Can you complete the work detailed in the bulleted doing tasks for this learning target? Prove it here.

Rate Your Current Level of Understanding				
1	**2**	**3**	**4**	**5**

Grades Earned on Assignments and Assessments

Additional Resources
Knowing Students Are Learning

Learning Target	Can you complete the work detailed in the bulleted doing tasks for this learning target? Prove it here.

Rate Your Current Level of Understanding

1	2	3	4	5

Grades Earned on Assignments and Assessments

Essential Vocabulary to Master

☐	☐	☐	☐	☐
☐	☐	☐	☐	☐
☐	☐	☐	☐	☐
☐	☐	☐	☐	☐

Additional Resources
Knowing Students Are Learning

The Big Book of Tools for Collaborative Teams in a PLC at Work © 2020 Solution Tree Press • SolutionTree.com
Visit **go.SolutionTree.com/PLCbooks/BBTCT** and enter the unique access code found on the book's inside front cover to access this reproducible.

Sample: Unit Overview Sheet for Student Self-Assessment in Upper Elementary, Middle, and High School

Name:

Unit: Eighth-Grade Economics

Over the next three weeks, we'll be studying economics. Specifically, we'll be studying the three key concepts of economics: (1) supply and demand, (2) budgeting, and (3) comparison shopping.

Essential Questions

☐ How do we make good financial decisions?	☐ How are the prices of goods and services determined?	☐ What impact does scarcity have on the price of a good or a service?
☐ What factors other than price impact the demand for a good or a service?	☐ What are the characteristics of a good budget?	☐ What are the best strategies for managing our finances in the short term and the long term?

Learning Target	**Can you complete the work detailed in the bulleted doing tasks for this learning target? Prove it here.**
I understand the law of supply and demand. This means I can explain how changes in demand will affect the supply or availability of a good or a service. This means I can also explain how the law of supply and demand affects the price of a good or a service. **Test your knowledge:** ☐ Can you explain why the price of ice might go up during natural disasters? ☐ Can you explain what would happen to the price of shovels if a snowstorm is coming? ☐ Can you describe how your business decisions would be different if you owned a service shoveling driveways in Vermont versus Virginia?	

Rate Your Current Level of Understanding

1	2	3	4	5

Grades Earned on Assignments and Assessments

page 1 of 3

Learning Target	Can you complete the work detailed in the bulleted doing tasks for this learning target? Prove it here.
I can create and maintain an individual budget. This means I can identify wants versus needs in an adjustable budget. This also means that I can use incoming revenue and outgoing expenses to create a balanced budget for one month. Finally, this means that I can explain the advantages and disadvantages of the four main actions people take with disposable income: (1) buying, (2) saving, (3) investing, and (4) donating. **Test your knowledge:** ☐ Can you track your income and expenses over a period of time? ☐ Given a failed monthly budget, can you identify and then fix the causes of a deficit? ☐ Given a sum of money, can you make a chart detailing how you will buy things with, save, invest, and donate those funds, and then give a rationale for each of your choices?	

Rate Your Current Level of Understanding				
1	**2**	**3**	**4**	**5**

Grades Earned on Assignments and Assessments				

The Big Book of Tools for Collaborative Teams in a PLC at Work © 2020 Solution Tree Press • SolutionTree.com
Visit **go.SolutionTree.com/PLCbooks/BBTCT** and enter the unique access code found on the book's inside front cover to access this reproducible.

Learning Target	Can you complete the work detailed in the bulleted doing tasks for this learning target? Prove it here.
I can make comparisons between the price, quality, and features of goods and services. This means I can make an accurate value versus cost determination between two different goods or services. **Test your knowledge:** ☐ Can you make a feature comparison table comparing the price, quality, and features of a school lunch versus a McDonald's meal? ☐ Can you make a feature comparison table comparing the price, quality, and features of Netflix versus Hulu? ☐ Can you make a feature comparison table comparing the price, quality, and features of _____ versus _____? ☐ Can you summarize how a cost-benefit analysis benefits a consumer?	

Rate Your Current Level of Understanding				
1	**2**	**3**	**4**	**5**

Grades Earned on Assignments and Assessments				

Essential Vocabulary to Master

☐ Supply	☐ Demand	☐ Wants	☐ Needs	☐ Budget
☐ Revenue	☐ Expenses	☐ Goods	☐ Services	☐ Buy
☐ Save	☐ Invest	☐ Donate	☐ Opportunity Cost	☐ Cost
☐ Value	☐ Cost-Benefit Analysis	☐ Price	☐ Equilibrium Price	☐ Deficit
☐ Surplus	☐ Consumer	☐	☐	☐

The Big Book of Tools for Collaborative Teams in a PLC at Work © 2020 Solution Tree Press • SolutionTree.com
Visit **go.SolutionTree.com/PLCbooks/BBTCT** and enter the unique access code found on the book's inside front cover to access this reproducible.

Tool: Evidence of Practice in Action

Instructions: In the first column, write a short description of each of the key instructional practices that your learning team members implement in their classrooms. In the second column, describe the steps that you have taken to document the effectiveness of each key instructional practice and the conclusions you have drawn from team data sets. And in the last column, indicate the action your team plans to take based on your findings.

Key Instructional Practice	Evidence of Impact	Next Steps
Sample: Our team has students annotate selections of text while reading, hoping that by slowing the reading process down, student comprehension will increase.	**Sample:** On the last two reading comprehension quizzes, students were required to annotate before answering any questions. The average score on these assessments increased by four points.	☑ Practice has proven to be successful and should be replicated. ☐ Practice needs continued study because the data collected point to inconsistent conclusions. ☐ Practice has no impact on student growth and should be eliminated.
		☐ Practice has proven to be successful and should be replicated. ☐ Practice needs continued study because the data collected point to inconsistent conclusions. ☐ Practice has no impact on student growth and should be eliminated.
		☐ Practice has proven to be successful and should be replicated. ☐ Practice needs continued study because the data collected point to inconsistent conclusions. ☐ Practice has no impact on student growth and should be eliminated.

Additional Resources — Knowing Students Are Learning

		<ul><li>☐ Practice has proven to be successful and should be replicated.</li><li>☐ Practice needs continued study because the data collected point to inconsistent conclusions.</li><li>☐ Practice has no impact on student growth and should be eliminated.</li></ul>
		<ul><li>☐ Practice has proven to be successful and should be replicated.</li><li>☐ Practice needs continued study because the data collected point to inconsistent conclusions.</li><li>☐ Practice has no impact on student growth.and should be eliminated.</li></ul>

Source: Adapted from Graham, P., & Ferriter, W. M. (2010). Building a Professional Learning Community at Work: A guide to the first year. *Bloomington, IN: Solution Tree Press.*

Tool: Evidence of Practice in Action—Teacher Self-Reflection

Step 1: Determine Your Current Self-Rating

Instructions: Circle a rating to show your current comfort level with the key instructional practice your team is studying. Remember to update this rating by erasing and recircling as you continue to use the key practice in your classroom.

Name of Key Instructional Practice: _____

Beginning	Mastering	Excelling
I understand the rationale for this instructional practice and have a basic idea of how to implement it in my classroom, but I'm not confident when using it in lessons with my students yet.	I am comfortable with this instructional practice and use it with regularity in my classroom. I think of it often while planning and can easily adapt it to new lessons. I've gotten great results when using this strategy with my students.	Not only do I use this instructional practice with regularity, but also I am experimenting with revisions that might make it even more effective. I have tried my revisions a few times and am collecting data to see if they are worth sharing with the entire team.

Step 2: Record Your Attempts With This Key Instructional Practice

Instructions: Add a new reflection each time that you use this key instructional practice in your classroom with your students. Then use the reflection questions at the end of this table to help you determine how to move forward.

Date of Attempt and Name of Lesson	What Went Well	What Could Be Improved
When did you use this key practice in your classroom? What concept were you teaching? What lesson were you delivering?	Did you prepare materials in a way that was particularly effective? Did you give directions differently than usual? Did you ask a good question? How did you monitor student learning?	Were there moments where students struggled with the key practice? Were there moments where you struggled? What caused those struggles? How would you change your approach next time?

The Big Book of Tools for Collaborative Teams in a PLC at Work © 2020 Solution Tree Press • SolutionTree.com
Visit **go.SolutionTree.com/PLCbooks/BBTCT** and enter the unique access code found on the book's inside front cover to access this reproducible.

Questions for Reflection

Are you getting better at using this key instructional practice in your classroom? How do you know? Was there a moment when you knew that you were beginning to use this practice effectively in your classroom? What was that moment?

How are other teachers on your learning team doing with this key instructional practice? Is anyone struggling to use it with his or her students? What help can you offer? Is anyone using it more effectively than you are? What can you learn from that person?

Have you gathered feedback from students about this key instructional practice yet? How do they feel about it? What suggestions have they made for improving the practice?

Tool: Practice-Centered Peer Observation

Instructions: Arrange to observe a peer teaching a lesson using one of your learning team's key instructional practices. Then, use the following tool—which includes questions that you should answer before your observation, during your observation, and after your observation—to document what you are learning about the key practice that you are observing. Remember, the focus of this observation is to improve your own understanding of how this key instructional practice can be implemented in classrooms.

Observer Name: _____

Peer to Observe: _____

Questions	Your Response
Questions to Answer *Before* Your Scheduled Observation	
What instructional practice are you planning to observe in your upcoming peer observation? • How do you implement this practice in your classroom? • Is there anything about your implementation that is unique or quirky? • Have you made any modifications to this instructional practice to fit your teaching style? Do you think those modifications have been successful?	
How would you rate the effectiveness of the instructional practice that you are planning to observe on a scale of 1 to 5, where 1 represents *very ineffective* and 5 represents *very effective*? • Is there anything about this instructional practice that you love? That you hate? • How do your students respond to this instructional practice? What do you think explains their response?	
Questions to Answer *During* Your Scheduled Observation	
How does your peer implement the instructional practice that you are observing? • Are there any unique phrases or directions that your peer uses to structure the activity for students that you hadn't considered? • Does your peer use body positioning or inflection in order to enhance the instructional practice in any way? • What about your peer's approach to this instructional practice will you try in your classroom?	

How do your peer's students respond to the instructional practice that you are observing?	
• Do they appear to be engaged and motivated? Do they appear to be struggling with the instructional practice in any way? • Does the instructional practice appear to be more effective for some students or student groups than others? How do you know? • Is the response of your peer's students to this instructional practice different from the response that you get from your own students? In what ways?	

Questions to Answer *After* Your Scheduled Observation

Have you learned anything new about this instructional practice, or about the needs of your students, during your observation?	
• What logical next steps can you and your team take in the development of this instructional practice? • Can you think of ways to tailor this instructional practice for students in need of remediation or enrichment? • Are there ways that this instructional practice can be used with different content or in different contexts? • Are there other learning teams that might benefit from what you have learned about this instructional practice?	

Final Thoughts and Next Steps

Source: Adapted from Ferriter, W. M., Graham, P., & Wight, M. (2013). Making teamwork meaningful: Leading progress-driven collaboration in a PLC. *Bloomington, IN: Solution Tree Press.*

Additional Resources
Knowing Students Are Learning

Tool: Understanding Common Assessment Strategies

Instructions: Together with your learning team, review the strengths and weaknesses of selected-response questions, constructed-response questions, and performance assessments. Then use the reflection questions to help you determine how you can use each most effectively.

Definitions of Popular Assessment Strategies
Selected-response items ask students to select the correct answer from provided information. Examples include multiple-choice questions, matching, and true–false questions (Ainsworth & Viegut, 2006; Popham, 2003; Stiggins, Arter, Chappuis, & Chappuis, 2004).
Constructed-response (also called *extended written-response* or *supply-response*) items ask students to provide their own answer to a question or prompt (Ainsworth & Viegut, 2006; Popham, 2003). While these include short-answer questions and essay responses, not all constructed-response questions involve writing. For example, teachers who ask their students to complete a graphic organizer (such as a Venn diagram) are using a constructed-response assessment.
Most assessment experts also recognize **performance assessments** as a type of assessment strategy (Ainsworth & Viegut, 2006; Stiggins et al., 2004). Marzano (2010) calls these *oral reports and demonstrations*. Performance assessments ask students to demonstrate their understanding of a learning target by performing in front of the teacher, who evaluates them against a rubric.

Questions for Reflection

Rank these assessment strategies in order from the most effective to the least effective. Do you think that teachers or teams teaching other grade levels and content areas would agree? Are some assessment strategies better suited for the content that you are required to teach? Why?

Which of these assessment strategies do you use the *most* frequently? What are its strengths? What are its weaknesses? Why do you turn to this assessment strategy so frequently?

Which of these assessment strategies do you use the *least* frequently? What are its strengths? What are its weaknesses? Why do you tend to avoid this assessment strategy?

Additional Resources
Knowing Students Are Learning

Source: Adapted from Bailey, K., & Jakicic, C. (2012). Common formative assessment: A toolkit for Professional Learning Communities at Work. *Bloomington, IN: Solution Tree Press.*

References

Ainsworth, L., & Viegut, D. (2006). *Common formative assessments: How to connect standards-based instruction and assessment.* Thousand Oaks, CA: Corwin Press.

Marzano, R. J. (2010). *Formative assessment and standards-based grading.* Bloomington, IN: Marzano Resources.

Popham, W. J. (2003). *Test better, teach better: The instructional role of assessment.* Alexandria, VA: Association for Supervision and Curriculum Development.

Stiggins, R. J., Arter, J. A., Chappuis, J., & Chappuis, S. (2004). *Classroom assessment for student learning: Doing it right—using it well.* Portland, OR: Assessment Training Institute.

Tool: Reflecting on the Dual Purposes of Common Formative Assessments

Instructions: Use the following claims by author and education leadership expert Kenneth C. Williams (2016) in tandem with the questions provided to reflect on the role that common formative assessments play in your building or on your learning team.

Questions	Your Response
Williams (2016) argues that there are *two primary purposes* for collecting common formative assessment data: (1) to identify students who are either struggling or excelling and (2) to help teachers improve their professional practice. Does your learning team—or the teams that you support—spend an equal amount of time on both of those purposes? If not, *which purpose is prioritized*? Why?	
Williams (2016) also asserts that instead of using common assessments to reflect on the effectiveness of their instructional practices, teachers and learning teams often make one another feel better for poor results by blaming the students. Do you agree with Williams? Is it a common practice for teachers to blame this year's group of students for results that don't meet expectations? How often does that happen in your school? Why do we slip into those kinds of unhealthy routines?	
Finally, Williams (2016) states that for teams to be able to use common formative assessment results in a meaningful way, *three conditions need to be in place*: (1) there must be strong levels of trust among members of a team, (2) administrators need to create a safe environment where data aren't used to shame or punish teachers, and (3) collaboration—particularly around data and instructional reflection—must be an expectation, not an option. Which of those conditions *currently exist* in your building? Which of those conditions do you control? What steps can you take today to strengthen the conditions under your control?	

Reference

Williams, K. C. (2016, August 17). How to use common formative assessments to help teachers reflect on practice *[Video file]*. Accessed at https://youtube.com/watch?v=9p3Fp5rBdz8 on August 5, 2019.

Checklist: Rating Your Team's Common Formative Assessment Practices

Instructions: Circle one rating for each row. Then record steps that you can take to improve your practice in the last column.

Rating Key

1 = We haven't tackled this yet.

2 = We are developing or refining our work in this area.

3 = This is an established practice for our team.

Your Rating			Key Indicator	Next Steps
1	2	3	Our team has come to an agreement on the value of common formative assessments and how we will use the data that we collect.	
1	2	3	Our team has identified power standards or essential learning targets and determined when they will be taught across the year.	
1	2	3	Our team has unpacked the power standards that we have identified in order to get up-front agreement on the specific skills and concepts we are trying to teach.	
1	2	3	Our team has a process for determining the quality of work or level of proficiency our students should meet in order to demonstrate mastery.	
1	2	3	Our common formative assessments are designed to monitor student understanding on just a few key learning targets at a time.	
1	2	3	Our common formative assessments contain an appropriate number of items (three to five per power standard) to effectively assess learning.	
1	2	3	Our team administers common formative assessments on a frequent basis in order to closely monitor and support student attainment of critical skills and concepts.	
1	2	3	Our team has a process to analyze the results of our common formative assessments in a timely fashion.	
1	2	3	Our team acts on the results of our common formative assessments in order to improve student learning.	
1	2	3	Our team engages students in the assessment process and provides meaningful feedback in a timely fashion.	

Source: © 2010 by Kim Bailey. Adapted with permission.

(sidebar) **Additional Resources** Knowing Students Are Learning

Survey: Data Literacy

Instructions: Working together with your collaborative peers, use the following survey to reflect on the data literacy of your learning team. Indicate the extent to which each of the following statements is true by circling one of the four ratings. Then, use the reflection questions at the end of the table to plan your next steps.

Rating Key

1 = Not true of our learning team
2 = Somewhat true of our learning team
3 = True of our learning team
4 = Very true of our learning team

Your Team: _____

Data Literacy Statement	Your Rating			
Our team has agreed-on expectations for mastery on most assignments.	1	2	3	4
Our team has developed our own set of common assessments that we use regularly (at least monthly).	1	2	3	4
Our common assessments are tied to state standards and are reliable measures of what students should know and be able to do.	1	2	3	4
Our team has developed our own set of common rubrics and exemplars that we can use to score performance-related tasks.	1	2	3	4
Our team has established an effective system for recording results from our common assessments.	1	2	3	4
Our team has an effective process for looking at the results of common assessments together.	1	2	3	4
Our team uses graphs and charts to make student achievement trends visible in our conversations about results.	1	2	3	4
Our team makes predictions about student learning based on common assessment results.	1	2	3	4
Our team changes our instructional practices based on common assessment results.	1	2	3	4
Our team provides remediation and extension to students based on common assessment results.	1	2	3	4
I feel safe when revealing my common assessment data in front of my peers.	1	2	3	4
Our team has a sense of shared responsibility for the success of all our students.	1	2	3	4
Our team has the skills necessary to collect and manipulate data effectively.	1	2	3	4
I know the difference between formative and summative assessments and understand when to use each.	1	2	3	4
Our team is aware of all the varied populations we serve and looks at results for each of these populations individually.	1	2	3	4
Our team has created systems for engaging students in data collection for self-assessment.	1	2	3	4

Additional Resources
Knowing Students Are Learning

Questions for Reflection

Please take a few moments to share any final thoughts about the use of data on your learning team. What are you proudest of? What are you the most concerned about? What are the most significant barriers preventing your team from using data more effectively? What kinds of resolutions can you imagine for overcoming those barriers?

Source: Adapted from Graham, P., & Ferriter, W. M. (2010). Building a Professional Learning Community at Work: A guide to the first year. *Bloomington, IN: Solution Tree Press.*

How Will We Respond When Some Students Don't Learn?

Think back for a minute about the steps that learning teams take while answering the first and second critical questions of learning in a PLC at Work: *What do we want our students to learn?* and *How will we know that they are learning it?* (DuFour et al., 2016). Together, teams identify the knowledge, skills, and dispositions that students must master in order to be successful. And together, they develop detailed plans for monitoring the progress that students are making toward mastering those essential outcomes. Both actions can have a powerful impact on *teachers*, providing focus for their collaborative efforts. Teams that develop a guaranteed and viable curriculum and common formative assessments have everything that they need in order to study their practice together in continuous cycles of collective inquiry.

Collaborative teams, however, recognize that the end goal of collaboration isn't just to study practice together. Instead, the end goal of collaboration is to *use the shared study of practice to ensure high levels of learning for all students*. And if we want to ensure high levels of learning for all students:

> we must be prepared with additional time and support for every student that demonstrates the need. Invariably, some students will need some extra help from time to time, while a few students will require a lot of extra help nearly every day. In other words, we must be prepared with a system of interventions designed to meet the unique needs of each child. (Buffum et al., 2012, p. 129)

Explicitly structuring a system of interventions that meets the unique needs of each student starts when collaborative teams answer the third and fourth critical questions of learning in a PLC at Work: *How will we respond when some students don't learn?*

and *How will we extend learning for students who are already proficient?* (DuFour et al., 2016). Answering these questions together has a powerful impact on *learners*, eliminating inequity by guaranteeing that every student, regardless of teacher, learns at the highest levels. The information and ideas included in this chapter are designed to help teams plan their intervention efforts for question 3 students—students who are struggling to master essential outcomes. Chapter 5 provides tools for planning extensions for question 4 students—students who are ready to move beyond the outcomes that a team has identified as essential.

Collaborative teams target their intervention efforts *by student* and *by cause* (DuFour et al., 2016) because they know that there are lots of different reasons that students need additional time and support for learning. Some students need extra chances to practice with, or different ways to demonstrate mastery of, grade-level essentials. Some haven't yet mastered the prerequisite knowledge or skills necessary for understanding grade-level curriculum. Some are still developing the work habits, attendance patterns, or social skills required for succeeding in school (DuFour et al., 2016). By working deliberately to provide *the right intervention to the right student at the right time*—instead of delivering the same intervention to every struggling student all at once—collaborative teams take an important step toward meeting the challenge of ensuring high levels of learning for all.

So how do collaborative teams make intervention by student and by cause doable? They start by focusing their time, energy, and effort on, and accepting primary responsibility for, helping students master the small set of essential outcomes detailed in their guaranteed and viable curriculum (Buffum, Mattos, & Malone, 2018). Stated more simply, collaborative teams develop and deliver interventions *only for the need-to-knows in their grade-level curriculum.* It is not necessary to plan interventions for outcomes that are not essential for students to master, and more intensive interventions for students who struggle with basic literacy and numeracy skills or who need significant behavioral or attendance support are most often developed and delivered by professionals with higher levels of training and expertise in the third tier of a school's response to intervention pyramid (Buffum et al., 2018).

Collaborative teams also make intervention by student and by cause doable by remembering that an intervention around grade-level essentials doesn't have to be complicated. Instead, "an intervention is anything a school does, above and beyond what all students receive, that helps a child succeed in school" (Buffum et al., 2012, p. 130). That means the second-grade team developing a series of short minilessons on common consonant blends to help students struggling to read, the fifth-grade social studies teachers developing opportunities for students struggling with written expression to create video responses as demonstrations of mastery of specific concepts, and the high school foreign language teachers asking students struggling with new syntax skills to review lessons in popular language learning apps like Duolingo or Babbel *are all providing interventions*. Collaborative teams recognize that they aren't competing to develop the most complex intervention plans. Instead, they are trying to identify a small handful of strategies that meet identified patterns of student need, can be easily adapted from unit to unit, and have a proven track record—either in the broader education community or with the students in their classrooms—of helping more students learn at higher levels.

Creating a Team-Based Intervention Plan for Struggling Students

While interventions for struggling learners don't have to be complicated in order to be successful, they do have to be deliberately planned and delivered based on the unique needs of every student. Deliberately planning and delivering interventions based on the unique needs of every student starts when teams understand that learners struggle to master essential outcomes for four main reasons.

1. **They have gaps in prerequisite learning:** Some students in need of intervention on your grade level are going to be missing the foundational knowledge or skills necessary to master the essential outcomes that you are currently teaching.

2. **They need additional practice:** Other students in need of intervention on your grade level will make common mistakes with the essential outcome that you are currently teaching. These mistakes can be easily corrected with a few opportunities for additional practice.

3. **They would benefit from alternative demonstrations of mastery:** Sometimes the students in need of intervention on your grade level aren't struggling with the concepts that you are asking them to master at all. Instead, they are struggling with the specific task that you are asking them to complete. These students would benefit from an opportunity to demonstrate mastery in a different way.

4. **They need support with work behaviors:** Finally, there will be students on your grade level who struggle to master the essential outcomes that you are currently teaching because they haven't yet mastered important work behaviors like completing homework assignments, participating in lessons, or coming to class prepared.

Teams cannot ensure high levels of learning for all until they have identified the specific strategies that they are going to use to support students struggling for each of these four reasons. Use the template on page 162 with your learning team to develop a comprehensive intervention plan and to maintain an up-to-date list of students who need continued support to master essential outcomes—essential steps for intervening by student and by cause.

Resources for Responding When Some Students Don't Learn

The resources in this chapter are all designed to help your learning team strengthen your intervention practices. The five fundamentals for responding when some students don't learn include the following.

1. **"Tool: Prerequisites and Extensions for an Essential Outcome"** (page 157)—Collaborative teams recognize that effective and efficient remediation and extension depend on having a clear sense of the prerequisite knowledge that students must have *before* they can master an essential outcome and the next steps that students will take *after* mastering an essential outcome. Use this template to think through the prerequisites and extensions for one of the essential outcomes that you are about to teach.

2. **"Tool: Tier 2 Intervention Tracking by Individual Teacher"** (pages 158–161)—Collaborative teams accept responsibility for helping *all* students master the outcomes they have identified as essential for future success. Sometimes, helping students master grade-level essentials requires teachers to take additional action after providing core instruction to their classes. These additional actions are called *Tier 2 interventions*. While teaching, use this template to keep track of the type of interventions that the struggling students in your classroom are likely to need in order to master essential outcomes.

3. **"Tool: Team-Based Intervention Plan for Struggling Students"** (page 162)—Collaborative learning teams recognize that to ensure high levels of learning for all students, they must identify students who are struggling with grade-level essentials *by name* and *by need*. They also understand that to ensure equity, the interventions offered to learners need to be planned together and delivered to all students regardless of teacher. Use this template to begin building an intervention plan to meet the specific needs of the students on your learning team.

4. **"Tool: List of Common Misconceptions for an Essential Outcome"** (page 163)—One of the best ways for learning teams to target their intervention work is to maintain lists of the common misconceptions and mistakes that students make when working with essential outcomes. By maintaining lists of common misconceptions and mistakes, teams can focus their

interventions on specific gaps in student learning. Use this template to track misconceptions for an essential learning outcome you are teaching.

5. **"Tool: Rating the Effectiveness of Interventions on Your Learning Team"** (page 164)—Collaborative learning teams are committed to taking action to ensure that all students are mastering essential outcomes. Those efforts depend on a team's ability to identify, document, and replicate intervention practices that work. Use this template to document the impact of the intervention practices that your learning team has chosen to embrace.

The additional resources for responding when some students don't learn are as follows.

- **"Tool: Individual Student Intervention Report"** (pages 166–167)—In *Learning by Doing*, DuFour et al. (2016) argue that schools should create a "timely, mandatory process to have staff members identify students for interventions" (p. 166). Use this template to create a detailed report for each student who is still struggling to master grade-level essentials after receiving first-best instruction and initial attempts at reteaching.

- **"Tool: Quarterly Work Behaviors Student Self-Assessment"** (pages 168–169)—As emphasized throughout this chapter, it is important to remember that students struggle in school for a variety of reasons. One reason that students struggle is because they haven't yet developed the kinds of positive work behaviors—coming to class prepared, completing assignments on time, participating in class discussions, asking for help when it is needed—that successful people demonstrate. Use this template to help students assess their own progress toward mastering those behaviors.

- **"Tool: Tracking Student Work Behaviors"** (pages 170–171)—Effectively addressing students' gaps in essential work behaviors like coming to class prepared, completing assignments on time, participating in class discussions, and asking for help when it is needed can begin only after teachers identify students who are struggling by name and by need. Use this performance tracking template to keep a record of the students in your classroom who need extra help to master essential work behaviors.

- **"Tool: Intervention Plan for Student Work Behaviors"** (page 172)—Just as with any other outcome, collaborative teams develop specific strategies for teaching essential work behaviors to their students. They also have a deliberate plan in place for providing additional time and support to students who are struggling to master essential work behaviors. Use this template to help your team develop an intervention plan for student work behaviors.

- **"Tool: Tier 2 Intervention Tracking by Learning Team"** (page 173)—Collaborative teams are constantly looking for patterns in their work, knowing that addressing patterns can make them more efficient and effective. After all the members of your team have used the "Tier 2 Intervention Tracking by Individual Teacher" template (page 158) to gather data on the students struggling to master grade-level essentials in their own classrooms, use this template to spot patterns in the intervention needs of students across your entire learning team. This tool is followed on page 174 by a sample designed to help you see how it can be used.

- **"Tool: Behavioral Analysis Protocol"** (pages 175–177)—Sometimes, persistent misbehavior is the greatest barrier to higher levels of learning for students in our classrooms. Intervening in these circumstances depends on teams that can competently diagnose the causes for persistent misbehavior and plan a series of next steps designed to help struggling students learn the behavioral skills necessary for succeeding in school. Use this Behavioral Analysis Protocol from *Simplifying Response to Intervention* (Buffum et al., 2012) to structure your team's next conversation about a student's persistent misbehavior.

- **"Tool: Creating a Record of Student Observations"** (pages 178–179)—One point to remember about interventions in a PLC is that teacher observations can be a valuable source of information about student levels of mastery. The key, however, is keeping a record of observations that the teacher can refer to when trying to determine next steps worth taking. Use this template to create an ongoing record of student observations that can be used to plan interventions for your students.

- **"Tool: Using Where Am I Going? Checklists to Differentiate Learning Experiences"** (page 180)—When teachers are the sole providers of feedback to learners, differentiated learning experiences are almost impossible to pull off. There are simply too many students to allow teachers to give timely and directive feedback to everyone on an as-needed basis. Collaborative teams can address this challenge by creating Where Am I Going? checklists for every unit. Where Am I Going? checklists provide students with a simple tool they can use to monitor their own progress toward mastering important outcomes. Use this template to create a Where Am I Going? checklist for one of your upcoming units by listing three to five essential outcomes, tasks that students can use as evidence to assess their progress, and specific actions students can take to move their own learning forward. Remember to use student-friendly language, and make sure that students can clearly understand your items. This tool is followed on page 181 by a sample checklist.

- **"Tool: Assessment Analysis Form"** (page 182)—Another step that teachers can take to empower students as partners in the intervention process is to ask students to complete an assessment analysis form after every common formative assessment (Ferriter & Cancellieri, 2017). Assessment analysis forms list the essential outcomes covered on an assessment, identify individual questions that are tied to each outcome, and provide students with a chance to reflect on their performance. Use this template to create an assessment analysis form for one of your upcoming common formative assessments. This tool is followed on page 183 by a sample designed to help you see how it can be used.

- **"Checklist: Rating Your Team's Intervention Practices"** (page 185)— Collaborative teams recognize that if they are going to successfully make the shift from *studying* their practice to *using* the shared study of practice to ensure high levels of learning for all students, they must develop intervention plans that are systematic and focused on the unique needs of every learner. Use this checklist to reflect on the intervention efforts of your learning team.

Five Fundamental Resources

for Responding When Some

Students Don't Learn

Tool: Prerequisites and Extensions for an Essential Outcome

Instructions: Complete one planning template for each of the essential outcomes that you will cover in your upcoming unit of study. Record in student-friendly language the essential outcome you are preparing to teach. Then, in the **Prerequisites** and **Extensions** columns, respectively, fill in the knowledge, skills, and vocabulary that students need before they can master this outcome and those that they can begin to study after they have mastered this outcome. Finally, use the reflection questions to help you determine next steps worth taking.

Essential Outcome Every Student Is Expected to Master:	
Prerequisites	**Extensions**

Questions for Reflection

Which prerequisites are students most likely to struggle with?

Which extensions are the most logical next steps for your students to explore?

What materials do you already have in place that you can use for reinforcing prerequisites or extending learning?

The Big Book of Tools for Collaborative Teams in a PLC at Work © 2020 Solution Tree Press • SolutionTree.com

Visit **go.SolutionTree.com/PLCbooks** to download this free reproducible.

Five Fundamental Resources
Responding When Some Students Don't Learn

Tool: Tier 2 Intervention Tracking by Individual Teacher

Instructions: Over the course of the next unit of study, record the names of students who are struggling to master essential outcomes. Use the second column to keep track of the essential outcomes that each student has yet to master. In the third column, check one box to indicate the type of intervention that would have the greatest impact on this student, and in the last column, record the actions that you will take to intervene on behalf of each student. Finally, use the reflection questions to spot patterns in the outcomes that your students are struggling with and to begin planning the interventions that they need.

Name of Unit:

Name of Student Who Is Struggling to Master Essential Outcomes	Essential Outcomes Student Is Struggling to Master	Primary Type of Intervention Student Needs	Your Next Actions
		☐ Support with prerequisite learning ☐ Additional practice ☐ Alternative ways to demonstrate mastery ☐ Support for work behaviors (completing tasks, planning long-term projects, coming to class prepared, being organized) ☐ Support for attendance or social skills ☐ Other:	

☐ Support with prerequi-
site learning

☐ Additional practice

☐ Alternative ways to
demonstrate mastery

☐ Support for work behav-
iors (completing tasks,
planning long-term
projects, coming to class
prepared, being organized)

☐ Support for attendance or
social skills

☐ Other:

☐ Support with prerequi-
site learning

☐ Additional practice

☐ Alternative ways to
demonstrate mastery

☐ Support for work behav-
iors (completing tasks,
planning long-term
projects, coming to class
prepared, being organized)

☐ Support for attendance or
social skills

☐ Other:

Five Fundamental Resources
Responding When Some Students Don't Learn

Name of Student Who Is Struggling to Master Essential Outcomes	Essential Outcomes Student Is Struggling to Master	Primary Type of Intervention Student Needs	Your Next Actions
		☐ Support with prerequisite learning ☐ Additional practice ☐ Alternative ways to demonstrate mastery ☐ Support for work behaviors (completing tasks, planning long-term projects, coming to class prepared, being organized) ☐ Support for attendance or social skills ☐ Other:	
		☐ Support with prerequisite learning ☐ Additional practice ☐ Alternative ways to demonstrate mastery ☐ Support for work behaviors (completing tasks, planning long-term projects, coming to class prepared, being organized) ☐ Support for attendance or social skills ☐ Other:	

The Big Book of Tools for Collaborative Teams in a PLC at Work © 2020 Solution Tree Press • SolutionTree.com

Visit **go.SolutionTree.com/PLCbooks/BBTCT** and enter the unique access code found on the book's inside front cover to access this reproducible.

Five Fundamental Resources
Responding When Some Students Don't Learn

☐ Support with prerequisite learning

☐ Additional practice

☐ Alternative ways to demonstrate mastery

☐ Support for work behaviors (completing tasks, planning long-term projects, coming to class prepared, being organized)

☐ Support for attendance or social skills

☐ Other:

Questions for Reflection

Which essential outcomes are proving to be the most difficult for your students to master?

What patterns can you spot in the types of interventions needed by your students?

Who can you turn to for help when planning and providing necessary interventions for your students? Which colleagues have discovered better ways to teach these essential outcomes to students? What strategies are they using?

Tool: Team-Based Intervention Plan for Struggling Students

Instructions: Record the essential outcomes that you are currently teaching. Then, indicate the type of intervention that you are planning and outline your intervention plan in the provided space. Finally, list the students in each classroom who need this intervention. Remember that students struggle to master essential outcomes for different reasons. You will need to create a separate intervention plan for each of the reasons that the students of your learning team are struggling.

Essential Outcomes We Are Currently Teaching:

Type of Intervention We Are Planning

☐ **Support with prerequisite learning** for students with gaps in foundational knowledge and skills that are preventing them from mastering the essential outcomes that we are currently teaching

☐ **Additional practice** for students who are making common mistakes that are likely to be easily corrected with a few opportunities to work with the essential outcomes again

☐ **Alternative demonstrations of mastery** for students who are struggling with a specific task and who might be able to demonstrate mastery of an essential outcome in a different way

☐ **Support for work behaviors** for students who are struggling to master an essential outcome because they haven't yet developed the habits demonstrated by successful learners (for example, coming to class prepared, participating in classroom discussions, or completing homework)

Our Intervention Plan:

List the students in each class who are currently in need of this intervention.

Teacher:	Teacher:	Teacher:	Teacher:

Tool: List of Common Misconceptions for an Essential Outcome

Instructions: Complete one common mistake or misconception template for each of the essential outcomes that you will cover in your upcoming unit of study. In the first column, describe up to three misconceptions that prevent students from mastering this essential learning outcome, or mistakes that you see students making frequently when working with this essential learning outcome. In the second column, provide an example of what each misconception or mistake looks like to help your team spot it easily in work samples. Copy your sample from a student work product or create one together with your learning team. In the last column, record your planned strategy, answering the following questions.

- *What steps will you take when you see this misconception or mistake in student work samples?*

- *Do you have follow-up assignments or question sets for addressing this misconception or mistake? Different instructional language worth trying? Reminders worth sharing with students?*

Essential Learning Outcome We Are Monitoring:		
Common Misconception or Mistake	**Example of This Misconception or Mistake**	**Planned Strategy**

Tool: Rating the Effectiveness of Interventions on Your Learning Team

Instructions: Complete one tracking template for each of the intervention practices that your learning team experiments with. In a few short sentences, describe this intervention. What essential knowledge and skills was it designed to address? Then answer the questions in each column in order to fully outline the effectiveness of the intervention, the materials you used, and ways to use this intervention in the future. Finally, assign a rating to the intervention using the provided scale.

Intervention Practice:

Evidence of Effectiveness	Required Materials	Future Revisions and Applications
How do you know that this intervention was effective? What evidence have you collected to show that the intervention has impacted student learning in a positive way? Did the intervention work better for some students than others? Why?	What resources were necessary to ensure effective implementation of this intervention? Include physical materials, lessons, and any additional faculty members who helped with this intervention practice.	What changes can you make to improve this intervention practice? How easily could you adapt this intervention practice to address other essential knowledge and skill gaps?

Rate This Intervention Practice

1	2	3	4	5
This intervention was ineffective or difficult to implement. It isn't useful to our team and should be abandoned.	Despite showing signs of some promise, there are too many implementation challenges to make this intervention worthwhile.	This intervention has promise—but it is going to need significant revisions to remain part of our team's intervention plans.	This intervention was highly effective, and with a few simple revisions, it will be easy to implement. We should continue to polish and improve it.	This intervention was highly effective and easy to implement just as it is. We should find ways to adapt it to new situations.

Source: Adapted from Graham, P., & Ferriter, W. M. (2010). Building a Professional Learning Community at Work: A guide to the first year. *Bloomington, IN: Solution Tree Press.*

Additional Resources

for Responding When Some

Students Don't Learn

Tool: Individual Student Intervention Report

Instructions: Use this template to create a detailed report for all students who are still struggling to master essential standards in your current unit of study after receiving first-best instruction and initial attempts at reteaching. Start by recording the essential standards that they are still struggling to master and the specific type of support that they need in order to be successful. Finally, document your attempts at intervention, using a new row for each attempt.

Student Name:

Which essential standards is this student still struggling to master?

What type of support does this student need in order to be successful with these essential standards?

Check all that apply. Address each checkmark in the following Notes section.

- ☐ This student needs support with prerequisite learning.
- ☐ This student needs additional practice opportunities.
- ☐ This student needs alternative ways to demonstrate mastery.
- ☐ This student needs to develop positive work behaviors (completing tasks, planning long-term projects, coming to class prepared, being organized).
- ☐ This student needs support for attendance or social skills.
- ☐ Other:

Notes

Include any details that can help target interventions for this student. What specific prerequisite skills is this student missing? What work behaviors or social skills is this student struggling with? What lessons was this student absent for? What alternative methods for demonstrating mastery work best for this student?

Record of Interventions

Create an entry in the following section for each of the interventions provided to this student.

Date	Description of the Intervention Attempt *Did you reteach a prerequisite skill? Did you address a specific work behavior or social skill? Did you provide an extra practice task? Which one?*	Notes *How effective was this attempt at intervention? How do you know? What will you try next? Who can help you provide additional support to this student?*

Tool: Quarterly Work Behaviors Student Self-Assessment

Instructions: Being successful in school and in life depends on more than just being good at reading, writing, and arithmetic. Being successful in school and in life depends on developing good work habits too. This checklist is designed to help you think about which work habits you have already mastered and which work habits you are still learning to master. Once you have finished rating yourself, ask your parents to rate you. Then, hand this paper back in so your teacher can rate you as well.

Name:			
Rate student performance in each category on a scale from 1 to 5.			
Indicator While assessing your work habits, place a checkmark next to indicators that you think you have mastered and a star next to indicators that you would like to work on over the next quarter.	**Student Rating**	**Parent or Guardian Rating**	**Teacher Rating**
Prompt, Prepared, and Reliable ☐ Has consistently good attendance ☐ Is prepared and ready to work on time ☐ Brings necessary materials to class			
Positive, Cooperative, and Self-Disciplined ☐ Exhibits a positive attitude ☐ Follows oral and written directions ☐ Actively participates in class discussions and group work ☐ Demonstrates appropriate behaviors with others			
Thorough, Complete, and Responsible ☐ Finishes assignments and make-up work on time ☐ Works well without extra supervision ☐ Gives best effort to tasks and projects ☐ Produces neat work			
Independent, Self-Motivated, and Creative ☐ Seeks help if needed ☐ Suggests ideas for improvement ☐ Assumes leadership responsibilities ☐ Demonstrates ability to work and apply knowledge independently ☐ Uses time well ☐ Demonstrates enthusiasm and interest			

page 1 of 2

The Big Book of Tools for Collaborative Teams in a PLC at Work © 2020 Solution Tree Press • SolutionTree.com
Visit **go.SolutionTree.com/PLCbooks** to download this free reproducible.

Questions for Reflection

Are there any areas where your self-rating differs significantly from the rating of your parents or your teacher? What explains those differences?

Which of your parents' and teacher's ratings do you agree with? Which do you disagree with? Why?

What next steps are you going to take during the upcoming quarter to improve your work behaviors? What specific indicators are you going to focus on? What specific changes are you going to make to help you improve?

Source: Adapted from Canady, R. L. (2003, August). Rethinking your grading practices. *Paper presented at the Wake County Public Schools Professional Learning Seminar, Raleigh, NC.*

page 2 of 2

Additional Resources
Responding When Some Students Don't Learn

Tool: Tracking Student Work Behaviors

Instructions: Use the following boxes to record the initials of any student struggling to master essential work behaviors in each quarter. Finally, use the reflection questions to help you determine next steps worth taking.

Essential Work Behaviors	Quarter 1	Quarter 2	Quarter 3	Quarter 4
Prompt, Prepared, and Reliable				
Has consistently good attendance				
Is prepared and ready to work on time				
Brings necessary materials to class				
Positive, Cooperative, and Self-Disciplined				
Exhibits a positive attitude				
Follows oral and written directions				
Actively participates in class discussions and group work				
Demonstrates appropriate behaviors with others				
Thorough, Complete, and Responsible				
Finishes assignments and make-up work on time				
Works well without extra supervision				
Gives best effort to tasks and projects				
Produces neat work				

page 1 of 2

Independent, Self-Motivated, and Creative				
Seeks help if needed				
Suggests ideas for improvement				
Assumes leadership responsibilities				
Demonstrates ability to work and apply knowledge independently				
Uses time well				
Demonstrates enthusiasm and interest				

Questions for Reflection

Which work behaviors are your students struggling to master? Why do you think these work behaviors are difficult for your students?

How do the patterns in your data set compare to the patterns in the data sets collected by other teachers on your learning team? Are all your students, regardless of teacher, struggling with the same essential work behaviors? Why? Why not?

What next steps are you going to take to help more students master the work behaviors that your team has identified as essential?

Source: Adapted from Canady, R. L. (2003, August). Rethinking your grading practices. *Paper presented at the Wake County Public Schools Professional Learning Seminar, Raleigh, NC.*

The Big Book of Tools for Collaborative Teams in a PLC at Work © 2020 Solution Tree Press • SolutionTree.com
Visit **go.SolutionTree.com/PLCbooks/BBTCT** and enter the unique access code found on the book's inside front cover to access this reproducible.

Tool: Intervention Plan for Student Work Behaviors

Instructions: Listed in the first column are the four main types of work behaviors demonstrated by successful learners. Together with your team, list the specific steps that you are taking to teach each type of work behavior to your students. Then, develop a plan for providing additional time and support to students who struggle to master each type of work behavior.

Essential Work Behaviors	How are we currently teaching these essential behaviors to our students? Are our strategies working? How do we know?	What is our plan for providing extra support to students struggling to master these work behaviors?
Prompt, Prepared, and Reliable • Has consistently good attendance • Is prepared and ready to work on time • Brings necessary materials to class		
Positive, Cooperative, and Self-Disciplined • Exhibits a positive attitude • Follows oral and written directions • Actively participates in class discussions and group work • Demonstrates appropriate behaviors with others		
Thorough, Complete, and Responsible • Finishes assignments and make-up work on time • Works well without extra supervision • Gives best effort to tasks and projects • Produces neat work		
Independent, Self-Motivated, and Creative • Seeks help if needed • Suggests ideas for improvement • Assumes leadership responsibilities • Demonstrates ability to work and apply knowledge independently • Uses time well • Demonstrates enthusiasm and interest		

Source: Adapted from Canady, R. L. (2003, August). Rethinking your grading practices. *Paper presented at the Wake County Public Schools Professional Learning Seminar, Raleigh, NC.*

The Big Book of Tools for Collaborative Teams in a PLC at Work © 2020 Solution Tree Press • SolutionTree.com

Visit **go.SolutionTree.com/PLCbooks/BBTCT** and enter the unique access code found on the book's inside front cover to access this reproducible.

Tool: Tier 2 Intervention Tracking by Learning Team

Instructions: After each member of your team has completed the "Intervention Tracking by Individual Teacher" tool (page 158), use this tool to compile data at the team level. Start by entering each teacher name in the left column. Then record the number of students needing intervention, sorting first by essential outcome and then by type of intervention. Tally your team's totals. Finally, use the reflection questions to help you determine next steps worth taking.

Name of Unit:

Teacher Name	Number of Students Needing Interventions Sorted by Essential Outcome					Number of Students Needing Interventions Sorted by Need				
	Outcome 1	Outcome 2	Outcome 3	Outcome 4	Outcome 5	Prerequisite Learning	Additional Practice	Alternative Demonstrations	Work Behaviors	Attendance or Social Skills	Other:
Team Totals											

Questions for Reflection

Which grade-level essentials are proving to be difficult for your students to master? Why are these outcomes so challenging? Which teachers have discovered promising practices for teaching these outcomes to students? What strategies are they using?

What patterns can you spot in the types of interventions that your students need? How effective have you been at providing these interventions to your students? Who can you turn to for help with planning and providing interventions for your students?

The Big Book of Tools for Collaborative Teams in a PLC at Work © 2020 Solution Tree Press • SolutionTree.com

Visit **go.SolutionTree.com/PLCbooks/BBTCT** and enter the unique access code found on the book's inside front cover to access this reproducible.

Sample: Tier 2 Intervention Tracking by Learning Team

Instructions: After each member of your team has completed the "Intervention Tracking by Individual Teacher" tool (page 158), use this tool to compile data at the team level. Start by entering each teacher name in the left column. Then record the number of students needing intervention, sorting first by essential outcome and then by type of intervention. Tally your team's totals. Finally, use the reflection questions to help you determine next steps worth taking.

Name of Unit:

Teacher Name	Number of Students Needing Interventions Sorted by Essential Outcome						Number of Students Needing Interventions Sorted by Need					
	Outcome 1	Outcome 2	Outcome 3	Outcome 4	Outcome 5		Prerequisite Learning	Additional Practice	Alternative Demonstrations	Work Behaviors	Attendance or Social Skills	Other:
Mr. Rich	9	1	0	6	2		5	8	1	4	0	0
Mrs. Seeger	8	0	0	1	0		3	4	0	2	0	0
Mrs. Lightfoot	10	3	0	9	1		8	6	1	6	1	1
Team Totals	27	4	0	16	3		16	18	2	12	1	1

Questions for Reflection

Which grade-level essentials are proving to be difficult for your students to master? Why are these outcomes so challenging? Which teachers have discovered promising practices for teaching these outcomes to students? What strategies are they using?

These data suggest that our students are having the most trouble with outcomes 1 and 4. For outcome 1, there doesn't appear to be any teacher with strategies that are highly effective. We are going to have to rethink the way that we are teaching that outcome to students. For outcome 4, we should dig into the way that Mrs. Seeger is teaching that concept because she appears to have a strategy that is working well for our students.

What patterns can you spot in the types of interventions that your students need? How effective have you been at providing these interventions to your students? Who can you turn to for help with planning and providing interventions for your students?

These data suggest that the most common interventions that we are using in this unit are preparing students with prerequisite skills, giving students extra practice with our essential outcomes, and helping them achieve better work behaviors. That is good news because those are all interventions that we can take primary responsibility for and that we don't need any extensive help with. We might want to reach out to the sixth-grade teachers to see if they can do more work with the prerequisites that our students are struggling with. That might make it easier for us to teach this unit moving forward.

Tool: Behavioral Analysis Protocol

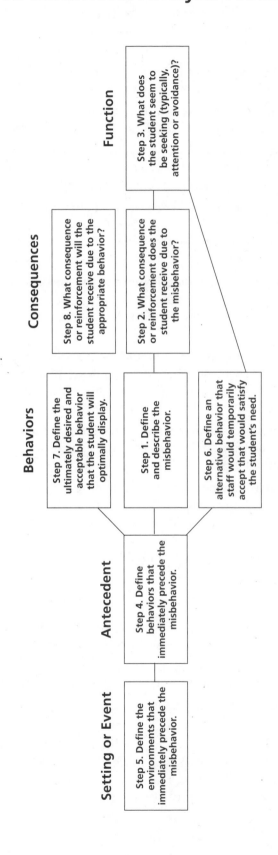

Setting or Event	Antecedent	Behaviors	Consequences	Function
Step 5. Define the environments that immediately precede the misbehavior.	Step 4. Define behaviors that immediately precede the misbehavior.	Step 7. Define the ultimately desired and acceptable behavior that the student will optimally display.	Step 8. What consequence or reinforcement will the student receive due to the appropriate behavior?	Step 3. What does the student seem to be seeking (typically, attention or avoidance)?
		Step 1. Define and describe the misbehavior.	Step 2. What consequence or reinforcement does the student receive due to the misbehavior?	
		Step 6. Define an alternative behavior that staff would temporarily accept that would satisfy the student's need.		

The Big Book of Tools for Collaborative Teams in a PLC at Work © 2020 Solution Tree Press • SolutionTree.com
Visit **go.SolutionTree.com/PLCbooks** to download this free reproducible.

Directions

A team can use this flowchart to help determine the causes of a student's misbehavior, and to help decide what types of behaviors would be accepted and preferred. We recommend that these steps be completed with, or at least communicated to, all stakeholders, including teachers, parents, and the student.

1. **Define and describe the misbehavior.** The team should describe the student's actions, words, and overall behavior as specifically as possible.

2. **What consequence or reinforcement does the student receive due to the misbehavior?** The team should detail what consequences the student has received as a result of the misbehavior.

3. **What does the student seem to be seeking (typically, attention or avoidance)?** Based on the team's responses in steps 1 and 2, as well as other knowledge of the student, what need does the misbehavior seem to be meeting (what is the function or purpose of the behavior)?

4. **Define behaviors that immediately precede the misbehavior.** Based on observations of the student when he or she has exhibited this misbehavior, describe as specifically as possible the student's actions, words, and overall behavior that occur before the unacceptable misbehavior. This will help staff predict the misbehavior in the future and provide precorrections.

5. **Define the environments that immediately precede the misbehavior.** The team should describe where the student is, with whom the student is, what task the student is completing (or attempting to complete), and so on. This will further help staff predict the misbehavior and provide precorrections.

6. **Define an alternative behavior that staff would temporarily accept that would satisfy the student's need.** This will be an interim step; staff will "allow" a student to behave in a way that satisfies the function identified in step 3 but that is also acceptable to staff. This behavior is not the ultimately desired behavior and will not be reinforced.

7. **Define the ultimately desired and acceptable behavior that the student will optimally display.** While step 6 will be temporarily acceptable, the staff communicate, explain, and model the desired, acceptable behavior that will ultimately be expected.

8. **What consequence or reinforcement will the student receive due to the appropriate behavior?** Based on a discovery of items, objects, or activities that motivate the student (items, objects, or activities for which the student is willing to work), the staff determine positive reinforcers that the student will earn if the appropriate behavior identified in step 7 is exhibited. The goal is to phase out these external reinforcers as soon as possible.

Here is an example of how a team might describe each step.

1. Brian pushes his supplies and papers off his desk and talks in an inappropriately loud voice when asked to work collaboratively with the members of his table team.

2. Brian receives verbal warnings and is sent to the back of the classroom or to the classroom next door if the acting out continues.

3. Brian seems to be seeking to avoid working on certain assignments or with certain students.

4. Brian fidgets in his seat, calls out off-task comments, gets out of his seat to sharpen a pencil (or throw a paper away), or begins "organizing" his desk or binder.

5. Brian seems to act out when asked to work collaboratively, particularly when the assignment involves reading and when team members have to work side by side to complete the task (in other words, each team member is not assigned a separate subtask). It occurs more in language arts and social studies than mathematics and science, and more in the morning than the afternoon.

6. If Brian feels frustrated by the task or his classmates, he may either take a two-minute break at the computer or, if necessary, complete an alternative assignment.

7. The expectation, which will be modeled, is for Brian to join his team promptly to work; he cannot be the last member to join; he needs to listen and make positive comments (no put-downs or complaining); and he needs to successfully, cooperatively, and promptly complete his portion of the task.

8. Brian likes working on the computer. If he meets the expectation as described in step 7, he will earn time on the classroom computer to play the mathematics facts game during recess. The teacher, the principal, Brian, and his mom will review the plan in three weeks to revise or set a higher expectation for Brian to meet before earning computer time.

Source: Buffum, A., Mattos, M., & Weber, C. (2012). Simplifying response to intervention: Four essential guiding principles. Bloomington, IN: Solution Tree Press.

Tool: Creating a Record of Student Observations

Instructions: During your daily instruction, use this form to keep track of any informal observations that you make that help you determine the current level of mastery of individual students in your classroom. In the first column, record the name of the student who you have observed. Then, circle the level of mastery that your observation demonstrated. In crafting your responses for **Teacher Notes**, consider the following questions.

- *Which essential outcomes have you observed this student demonstrating?*
- *Is this student making predictable mistakes with any essential outcomes?*
- *Has this student demonstrated mastery of concepts and skills that go beyond basic expectations?*
- *Can you see gaps in prerequisite learning that are causing this student to struggle?*

Essential Outcomes We Are Monitoring:

Student Name	Level of Performance Observed (Circle one.)				Teacher Notes
	Intervention	Approaching Expectations	Meeting Expectations	Exceeding Expectations	
	Intervention	Approaching Expectations	Meeting Expectations	Exceeding Expectations	
	Intervention	Approaching Expectations	Meeting Expectations	Exceeding Expectations	
	Intervention	Approaching Expectations	Meeting Expectations	Exceeding Expectations	

page 1 of 2

	Intervention	Approaching Expectations	Meeting Expectations	Exceeding Expectations		
	Intervention	Approaching Expectations	Meeting Expectations	Exceeding Expectations		
	Intervention	Approaching Expectations	Meeting Expectations	Exceeding Expectations		
	Intervention	Approaching Expectations	Meeting Expectations	Exceeding Expectations		
	Intervention	Approaching Expectations	Meeting Expectations	Exceeding Expectations		
	Intervention	Approaching Expectations	Meeting Expectations	Exceeding Expectations		

Rating Key

Exceeding expectations: Student demonstrates proficiency with concepts, skills, and behaviors that go beyond those required for mastering this essential learning outcome. Completes all assignments and assessments without errors and without support from teachers or classmates.

Meeting expectations: Student demonstrates proficiency with concepts, skills, and behaviors required for mastering this essential learning outcome. Completes assignments and assessments with few errors and with minimal support provided by teachers or classmates.

Approaching expectations: Student demonstrates inconsistent proficiency with concepts, skills, and behaviors required for mastering this essential learning outcome. Errors in assignments and assessments fit predictable patterns and can be addressed through additional practice.

Intervention: Student fails to demonstrate proficiency with concepts, skills, and behaviors required for mastering this essential learning outcome. Errors in assignments and assessments indicate significant conceptual misunderstandings that can only be addressed by direct action, instruction, or intervention from teachers.

Additional Resources
Responding When Some Students Don't Learn

Tool: Using Where Am I Going? Checklists to Differentiate Learning Experiences

Unit: _____

Instructions: Use this reflection sheet to track your progress.

Where Am I Going? What content and skills do I need to master during this unit? What key questions have I been wrestling with?	How Am I Doing? What evidence can I collect to track my progress toward mastering essential content and skills?	What Are My Next Steps? What steps can I take to continue my learning?
☐	☐	☐
☐	☐	☐
☐	☐	☐
☐	☐	☐

1. In the **Where Am I Going?** column, list three to five essential outcomes for this upcoming unit of study that are written in student-friendly language. Consider creating questions that students can answer with a clear yes or no response.

2. In the **How Am I Doing?** column, list three to five tasks that students can use as evidence to assess their own progress toward mastering the essential outcomes covered on this checklist.

3. In the **What Are My Next Steps?** column, list three to five specific actions that students can take to move their own learning forward. Students should be able to clearly understand these actions and require no additional direction from the teacher.

Source: Adapted from Ferriter, W. M., & Cancellieri, P. J. (2017). Creating a culture of feedback. Bloomington, IN: Solution Tree Press.

Sample: Where Am I Going? Checklist

(Note: This sample reflects what your team would create and hand out to students. Students would then fill in their own scores as they complete each activity.)

Unit: Over the past few weeks, we have been learning how to write a Claim-Evidence-Reasoning piece.

Instructions: Use this reflection sheet to track your progress.

Where Am I Going?	How Am I Doing?	What Are My Next Steps?
What content and skills do I need to master during this unit? What key questions have I been wrestling with?	What evidence can I collect to track my progress toward mastering essential content and skills?	What steps can I take to continue my learning?
☐ Can I make a clear statement of my *claim*—that is, my position on the topic that we are studying or question that we are answering?	☐ My score on *Identifying Convincing Evidence* activity:	☐ Review classroom Edpuzzle tutorials on using commas and semicolons in writing.
☐ Can I select convincing *evidence* (both qualitative and quantitative) to support my claim?	☐ My score on *Punctuate This* activity:	☐ Meet with a peer tutor during intervention period to rate and review the evidence that I have chosen for a classroom Claim-Evidence-Reasoning task.
☐ Can I include *reasoning* that explains how each piece of evidence that I have selected supports my claim?	☐ My score on *Is Percy Jackson and the Olympians: The Lightning Thief a Book Worth Reading?* activity:	☐ Complete the *My Dad Is an Alien* task to review the differences between qualitative and quantitative observations.
☐ Can I use standard punctuation and grammar in my writing, ensuring that people can understand what I am saying?	☐ My score on *Is Space Exploration Worth the Cost?* activity:	☐ Extend my learning about Claim-Evidence-Reasoning pieces by using the format to create a piece designed to convince my parents that they should buy me a new puppy as a pet.
	☐ Other evidence of your learning (questions answered in class, contributions to group projects, comparisons with the thoughts of partners):	☐ Ask this question in class to clarify something that I'm wondering or confused about: _____

Source: Adapted from Ferriter, W. M., & Cancellieri, P. J. (2017). Creating a culture of feedback. Bloomington, IN: Solution Tree Press.

Additional Resources
Responding When Some Students Don't Learn

Tool: Assessment Analysis Form

Instructions: Now that we have completed our assessment on _____, let's look carefully at the questions that you got right and that you got wrong. In the column labeled **Questions That Cover This Learning Target**, shade the boxes for all the questions that you answered correctly. Leave the questions answered incorrectly unshaded. Then, let's see if we can spot any patterns in the kinds of mistakes that you made on our assessment. Finally, let's sort the essential outcomes covered on this assessment into three categories: (1) **I've Mastered These Targets**, (2) **I Need a Quick Review of These Targets**, or (3) **These Targets Are Still Really Hard for Me**.

Student Name: _____

Learning Target Covered on This Assessment	Questions That Cover This Learning Target				

Reflection	
I've Mastered These Targets List the learning targets where you answered every question correctly on our recent assessment.	
I Need a Quick Review of These Targets List the learning targets where you made simple mistakes when answering questions incorrectly on our recent assessment.	
These Targets Are Still Really Hard for Me List the learning targets where you answered most questions incorrectly, or really struggled to come up with correct answers, on our recent assessment.	

Final Thoughts

Looking back at your performance on this assessment, are there reasons to celebrate? Are there new things that you've learned? What do you know now that you didn't know at the beginning of our unit? Is there evidence that you still have some work to do before being able to say that you've mastered the learning targets covered on this assessment? Are there concepts you don't understand yet? What are you still working to learn?

Source: Adapted from Ferriter, W. M., & Cancellieri, P. J. (2017). Creating a culture of feedback. *Bloomington, IN: Solution Tree Press.*

Sample: Assessment Analysis Form

Instructions: Now that we have completed our assessment on reading literature, let's look carefully at the questions that you got right and that you got wrong. In the column labeled **Questions That Cover This Learning Target**, shade all questions that you answered correctly. Leave the questions answered incorrectly unshaded. Then, let's see if we can spot any patterns in the kinds of mistakes that you made on our assessment. Finally, let's sort the essential outcomes covered on this assessment into three categories: (1) **I've Mastered These Targets**, (2) **I Need a Quick Review of These Targets**, or (3) **These Targets Are Still Really Hard for Me**.

Student Name: Latonya K.

Learning Target Covered on This Assessment	Questions That Cover This Learning Target			
1. **I can recognize the cumulative impact that word choice has on the tone of a story.** This means I can identify sets of words that, taken together, set a sense of time and place, a formal or informal tone, or the overall mood of a story..	1	2	3	4
2. **I can use textual evidence to analyze a story.** This means I can find specific pieces of evidence to support my claims about what a story explicitly says and make accurate inferences about what individual events in a story may mean.	5	6	7	
3. **I can explain how complex characters develop over the course of a text.** This means I can identify the motivations of a character and detail how those motivations influence both that character's interactions with other characters and the character's impact on the story.	8	9	10	

Reflection	
I've Mastered These Targets List the learning targets where you answered every question correctly on this assessment.	Target 2
I Need a Quick Review of These Targets List the learning targets where you made simple mistakes when answering questions incorrectly on this assessment.	Target 1
These Targets Are Still Really Hard for Me List the learning targets where you answered most questions incorrectly, or really struggled to come up with correct answers, on this assessment.	Target 3

Additional Resources
Responding When Some Students Don't Learn

page 1 of 2

Final Thoughts

Looking back at your performance on this assessment, are there reasons to celebrate? Are there new things that you've learned? What do you know now that you didn't know at the beginning of our unit? Is there evidence that you still have some work to do before being able to say that you've mastered the learning targets covered on this assessment? Are there concepts you don't understand yet? What are you still working to learn?

I think overall, I'm doing well as a reader. I can do most of the basic work that readers are required to. I don't have any trouble finding text evidence to identify exactly what a story is saying. I really like doing that. It feels like I am being a detective, trying to spot proof of my claims. I'm also doing well at figuring out how individual words impact the overall tone of a story. That's a lot like acting like a detective too.

I'm definitely struggling to identify how characters develop over the course of a story, though. I notice that this happens the most when characters act in surprising ways—or in ways that don't look a whole lot like the ways that my friends would act. In a lot of stories that we read, I was shocked by the choices made by characters. I didn't see their decisions coming. I have to remind myself when I am reading that not all characters are going to act in ways that I expect. That might help me spot clues to their motivations sooner.

Checklist: Rating Your Team's Intervention Practices

Instructions: Using the following key, circle your rating for each indicator. Then record your next steps in the last column.

Rating Key

1 = We haven't tackled this yet.
2 = We are developing or refining our work in this area.
3 = This is an established practice for our team.

Your Rating			Key Indicator	Next Steps
1	2	3	Our team has identified the prerequisite knowledge necessary to master each of our grade-level essentials.	
1	2	3	Our team has developed a list of common misconceptions or mistakes for each of our grade-level essentials.	
1	2	3	Our team has developed lessons that include opportunities for intervention, extra practice, and extension.	
1	2	3	*Individual teachers* have well-established systems of collecting information about the intervention needs of students that are sorted by name and by need.	
1	2	3	*Our team* keeps updated lists, sorted by name and by need, of students who require additional time or support.	
1	2	3	Our team has strategies for supporting students who haven't yet mastered essential work behaviors.	
1	2	3	Our team has a system for reporting on the specific intervention needs of individual students to parents and other professionals working beyond the classroom.	
1	2	3	Our team has identified a set of intervention strategies or practices that we believe in and that we know have a positive impact on student learning.	
1	2	3	Our team collects data on the intervention needs of our students and uses those data to identify strengths and weaknesses in our teaching practice.	
1	2	3	Our team has developed opportunities for students to track their own progress and to plan their next learning actions.	

The Big Book of Tools for Collaborative Teams in a PLC at Work © 2020 Solution Tree Press • SolutionTree.com

Visit **go.SolutionTree.com/PLCbooks/BBTCT** and enter the unique access code found on the book's inside front cover to access this reproducible.

Additional Resources
Responding When Some Students Don't Learn

How Will We Extend Learning When Students Are Already Proficient?

Portions of this chapter appear in
"Extending Learning in an #atplc School" (Ferriter, 2020).

For many learning teams, being prepared with additional time and support for every student who demonstrates the need means doing all that we can to help struggling students master essential outcomes (Buffum et al., 2012). And there's nothing fundamentally wrong with that thinking. If we truly believe that the outcomes we have identified for each unit of study are essential for success both in and beyond our classrooms, then we have nothing short of a *moral obligation* to make sure that all students—including those who struggle—master them. This moral obligation creates a sense of urgency around the work that we do for question 3 students. Schools use universal screening tests multiple times a year to identify specific skill gaps, and then they target those gaps during all-hands-on-deck intervention periods, where struggling students receive intensive support in their areas of greatest need; intervention experts meet with learning teams during regularly scheduled "kid talk" meetings designed to monitor the ongoing progress that struggling students are making toward mastering grade-level essentials; and teachers set aside planning minutes to design intervention lessons and instructional minutes to work in small groups with struggling students.

The highest-performing learning teams, however, recognize that our moral obligation isn't *only* to help all students master our essential outcomes. Instead, our moral obligation is to *help all students learn at the highest levels*. Even in the face of external pressure to decrease the number of students identified as nonproficient from year to year, collaborative teams work with the same urgency to extend the learning of students who have already demonstrated mastery of grade-level essentials as they do to intervene on behalf of students who are struggling (Roberts, 2019; Weichel, McCann, & Williams, 2018). Tier 2 interventions on collaborative teams, then—traditionally thought of as teacher-led efforts to provide supplemental help with grade-level essentials (DuFour et al., 2016)—also include extensions that are carefully designed to "take the learning beyond what the core instruction has provided" (Roberts, 2019, p. 20).

Extending the Learning With Care for Proficient Students

The highest-performing learning teams recognize that their students are unique individuals with differing skill sets. That means every student—regardless of perceived ability—is likely to need both intervention and extension at different points during a school year. Instead of thinking of question 4 students as the academically gifted students in our classrooms, collaborative teams see question 4 students as all the students in our classrooms who have demonstrated proficiency with the grade-level essentials that we are working on right now. That simple shift in thinking allows collaborative teams to look for the superior potential in every student and to break the dangerous cycle of targeting only the weaknesses that we see in our students—a cycle that disproportionately impacts those from poor communities or underachieving subgroups (Jackson, 2011). "When we believe in the vast intellectual capacity of all students to achieve at high levels," writes Yvette Jackson (2011) in *The Pedagogy of Confidence*, "we are relentless in searching for ways to unleash that capacity" (p. 53).

Relentlessly searching for ways to unleash the intellectual capacity of question 4 students starts when learning teams prioritize planning for extensions, recognizing that meeting the needs of students who are already proficient depends on something more than "fly-by-the-seat-of-your-pants teaching" (Roberts, 2019, p. 38). In fact, the highest-performing teams often *teach up*, a practice that involves "planning first for advanced learners, then scaffolding instruction to enable less advanced students to access those rich learning experiences" (Tomlinson, 2015). Doing so leads to more meaningful instruction and higher levels of achievement for all students (Tomlinson, 2015).

While there are many ways to plan extensions for advanced learners, three primary strategies are recommended in *Learning by Doing* (DuFour et al., 2016), the seminal text written by the original architects of the Professional Learning Community at Work movement.

1. **"Students can be asked to demonstrate mastery of essential standards at a level beyond what is deemed grade-level proficient" (DuFour et al., 2016, p. 170):** In most cases, curricula for different content areas have been carefully spiraled, exposing students to similar concepts at increasing levels

of complexity from year to year. Collaborative teams use these curricular spirals to create proficiency scales and rubrics that define multiple levels of mastery for each essential outcome. Then, they use these scales and rubrics to extend learning by asking question 4 students to demonstrate mastery at levels that go beyond grade-level proficiency.

2. **"Students can have access to more of the grade-level curriculum that is deemed important, but not essential" (DuFour et al., 2016, p. 170):** When working together to answer the first critical question of learning in a PLC (What do we want our students to learn?), collaborative teams divide the outcomes in their required curriculum into two simple categories: (a) need to knows and (b) nice to knows. *Need to knows* become the grade-level essentials that teams work together to ensure that every student learns. *Nice to knows* are nonessential outcomes that question 4 students can receive exposure to as part of extension tasks.

3. **"Students can be taught above grade-level curriculum" (DuFour et al., 2016, p. 170):** Learning in most content areas is progressional. The concepts and skills that students are introduced to this year are designed to prepare them for success in the same content area next year. As a result, effective teachers spend time studying what it is that students *have already learned* and what it is that students *are going to learn next*. High-performing learning teams use this knowledge of learning progressions in their curriculum to create extension tasks, giving question 4 students chances to wrestle with above-grade-level concepts and skills.

Michael Roberts (2019)—author of *Enriching the Learning: Meaningful Extensions for Proficient Students in a PLC at Work*—offers a fourth strategy worth considering.

4. Students can be asked **"to apply their learning on [an] extension standard to a real-life situation not addressed in class" (Roberts, 2019, p. 14):** Students of all ages have an inherent need to see value in the content and skills that they are being asked to master. Engagement, then, depends on ensuring that students have a clear sense of why their learning matters. Collaborative teams use this need for relevance to create extensions by introducing question 4 students to real-life examples of essential outcomes in action or by asking question 4 students to use the knowledge that they have learned to solve real-life problems.

Like the intervention efforts introduced in the previous chapter, collaborative teams make extending learning doable by remembering that extensions don't have to be complicated in order to be meaningful. The kindergarten team asking already proficient students to compare the basic shapes found in nature to the basic shapes found in the architecture of playground structures, the eighth-grade science teachers asking already proficient students to rank order pathogens from most dangerous to least dangerous, and the high school statistics teacher asking already proficient students to identify the inaccuracies in the data being shared by biased news sources *are all providing extensions.*

The key rests in remembering, however, that providing extensions for already proficient students means developing tasks that require students to work "thoughtfully at a deep cognitive level over an extended period of time" (Roberts, 2019, p. 2). Common practices like assigning more problems to already proficient students, allowing already proficient students to read quietly or work independently on other high-interest tasks, or asking already proficient students to serve as tutors to their struggling peers can have a negative social and academic impact on learners (Roberts, 2019). Students asked to engage in these practices on a regular basis quickly stagnate, realizing that their continued learning isn't a priority in the classroom—and teachers who lean heavily on these practices fail to meet the moral obligation to help all students learn at higher levels.

Resources for Extending Learning When Students Are Already Proficient

The resources in this chapter are all designed to help your learning team strengthen your extension practices. The five fundamentals for responding when some students need extensions include the following.

1. **"Tool: Analyzing Your Team's Extension Reality"** (page 195)—The first step toward strengthening your learning team's extension practices is to carefully analyze your current extension reality. How important do you think it is to provide extensions to question 4 students? How prepared are you to provide extensions to question 4 students? What support does your team need in order to make extending learning for question 4 students feel more doable? Use this template to think through those kinds of questions together with your learning team.

2. **"Tool: Extension Plan for a Unit of Study"** (page 196)—In *Taking Action*, Buffum et al. (2018) describe three different types of extension opportunities offered by learning teams: (a) asking students to demonstrate mastery of essential standards beyond grade-level proficiency, (b) giving students access to parts of the required grade-level curriculum deemed important but not essential, and (c) teaching students above-grade-level curriculum. Use this template to plan extension opportunities for an upcoming unit of study in each of those three areas.

3. **"Tool: Weekly Extension Planning Template"** (page 197)—The unfortunate truth is that conversations about extension are rarely prioritized by learning teams during their weekly collaborative meetings. The result: question 4 students become "at risk" because their unique learning needs are easily overlooked or quickly dismissed by teams that are pressed for time (Roberts, 2019; Weichel et al., 2018). To avoid falling into this trap, start each collaborative team meeting by using this simple template to record both the essential outcomes that you will be teaching in the upcoming week and your initial plans for providing extensions.

4. **"Tool: Using Proficiency Scales to Define Levels of Mastery"** (page 198)— If learning teams are going to *teach up*—first planning for advanced learners and then scaffolding instruction to allow all students to access higher levels of learning—they must first create clear definitions of just what high levels of learning look like in action. It is impossible to extend learning for students without having a shared understanding of the next steps that students can take to move forward, regardless of their current level of performance. In *Formative Assessment and Standards-Based Grading*, Marzano (2010) argues that the best way to define levels of mastery on a collaborative team is to develop proficiency scales for each essential outcome. Use this template to work through that process with your peers. This tool is followed on pages 199–202 by two samples that are designed to help you see how it can be used.

5. **"Tool: Using Depth of Knowledge Levels to Increase the Complexity of an Existing Task"** (page 204)—One of the easiest ways to create extensions for question 4 students is to ask them to demonstrate mastery of essentials at levels that go beyond grade-level proficiency. After referring to the key on page 203, use this template—which outlines Norman Webb's (1997) Depth of Knowledge levels—to increase the cognitive complexity of the tasks that you are already using as demonstrations of proficiency. Those revised tasks can then be used as extensions for students who are ready to move beyond grade-level essentials.

The additional resources for responding when some students need extensions include the following.

- **"Tool: Building Your Learning Team's Knowledge About Extensions"** (page 206)—To effectively extend learning, collaborative teams must possess a solid foundational understanding of some of the most common strategies used to extend learning: asking students to demonstrate mastery at levels beyond grade-level proficiency, giving students opportunities to study nonessential curriculum, teaching students above-grade-level curriculum, and introducing students to real-life examples of essential outcomes in action (DuFour et al., 2016; Roberts, 2019). Use this template to review each of those strategies and to reflect on your team's current extension practices.

- **"Tool: Developing a Tiered Lesson Plan"** (pages 207–209)—Collaborative teams recognize that there is a broad range of student abilities in every classroom and for every lesson. As a result, they deliberately plan tiered lessons that are designed to provide meaningful learning experiences for every student, regardless of ability. Use this template to begin planning a tiered lesson for one of the concepts in your curriculum.

- **"Tool: Developing a Tiered Task Card"** (page 210)—For many teachers, the logistics of providing differentiated tasks to students can be overwhelming. To address this logistical challenge, differentiation expert Carol Ann Tomlinson (2017) recommends creating *anchor activities*: tasks that students can automatically turn to after demonstrating proficiency with grade-level essentials. One way to communicate anchor activities to your students is to develop tiered task cards. These include a set of three different tasks that are tied to the same essential outcome, but that increase in cognitive complexity. Students can then turn to tiered task cards whenever they are ready for additional challenge. Use this template to create a tiered task card for an upcoming essential outcome. This tool is followed on page 211 by a sample that is designed to help you see how it can be used.

- **"Tool: Curriculum Compacting Contract"** (page 212)—Another strategy that learning teams can use to provide a differentiated learning experience for question 4 students is curriculum compacting. *Curriculum compacting* involves adjusting instruction for already proficient students by replacing content with extension options that go beyond grade-level expectations. Teams that use curriculum compacting as an extension task often develop a contract that can be used to provide clarity and direction for students engaged in the compacting experience (Weichel et al., 2018). Use this template to develop a curriculum compacting contract for your next unit of study. This tool is followed on page 213 by a sample that is designed to help you see how it can be used.

- **"Tool: Creating a Review Tutorial for an Essential Standard"** (pages 214–215)—Many collaborative teams leverage the power of technology to provide initial reteaching to students who need supplemental help with grade-level essentials by using free services like Edpuzzle (https://edpuzzle.com) to create review tutorials. This simple practice can easily be turned into an extension activity by asking your question 4 students to create review tutorials for their peers. This template can be used to guide already proficient students through that process.

- **"Tool: Using Student Wonder Questions as Extension Tasks"** (pages 216–217)—One of the lessons that teachers learn early in their careers is that students are almost always naturally curious, constantly generating interesting questions about the content they study in class. Turning these interesting questions into quick and easy extension tasks starts when teachers give students regular opportunities to record the things that they are wondering about during each unit of study. Ask your students to use this template to keep track of the questions that they want to find answers to.

- **"Tool: Tracking Real-Life Examples of Essential Outcomes in Action"** (pages 218–219)—In *Enriching the Learning*, extension expert Michael Roberts (2019) suggests that one way to create extensions is to ask question 4 students to apply their knowledge of essential outcomes to real-life situations. Learning teams can facilitate that work by maintaining updated lists of links to news stories where essential outcomes are reflected in happenings at the local, state, or national level. These lists can become resources that teachers turn to when trying to extend learning for question 4 students. Use this template to create a list of real-life extension opportunities for your next unit of study.

- **"Tool: Rating the Extensions on Your Learning Team"** (page 220)—High-performing learning teams are committed to taking action to ensure that all students are learning at the highest levels, including those who have already demonstrated proficiency with grade-level essential learning. Those efforts depend on a team's ability to identify, document, and replicate extension practices that work. Use this template to document the impact of the extension practices that your learning team has chosen to embrace.

- **"Tool: How Is Your Learning Team Spending Your Collaborative Time?"** (pages 221–222)—In *When They Already Know It*, authors Mark Weichel, Blane McCann, and Tami Williams (2018) argue that it is impossible for teams to strengthen their extension practices for question 4 students until they carefully reflect on the ways that they are already spending their collaborative time. Use this template—which is adapted from a series of reflection questions included in *When They Already Know It*—to start that conversation with your team.

- **"Checklist: Evaluating Your Team's Extension Practices"** (pages 223–224)—Collaborative teams recognize that if they are going to successfully make the shift from ensuring that all students *learn their essential outcomes* to ensuring that all students *learn at the highest levels,* they must be as committed to—and skilled with—extensions as they are with interventions. Use this checklist to evaluate the extension efforts of your learning team.

Five Fundamental Resources

for Extending Learning When

Students Are Already Proficient

Tool: Analyzing Your Team's Extension Reality

Instructions: For the first three questions in the following tool, work with your learning team to circle an indicator that best represents your current extension reality. Then, use the reflection questions at the bottom of this template to analyze your team's readiness to begin providing extensions for question 4 students.

Question 1: On a scale from 1 to 5, *how important* do you think it is for teams to provide extension opportunities to students who are already proficient with essential outcomes?

Not Important	1	2	3	4	5	Very Important

Question 2: On a scale from 1 to 5, *how often* does your team provide extension opportunities to students who are already proficient with essential outcomes?

Not Often	1	2	3	4	5	Almost Always

Question 3: On a scale from 1 to 5, *how prepared* do you feel to provide extension opportunities to students who are already proficient with essential outcomes?

Not Prepared	1	2	3	4	5	Very Prepared

Questions to Consider	Your Response
Why is it so important for learning teams to provide extension opportunities to students who are already proficient with essential outcomes?	
What challenges make it difficult for learning teams to provide extension opportunities to students who are already proficient with essential outcomes?	
What strengths does your team have when it comes to providing extension opportunities to students who are already proficient with essential outcomes?	
What support will your learning team need in order to make providing more extension opportunities to students who are already proficient doable?	

The Big Book of Tools for Collaborative Teams in a PLC at Work © 2020 Solution Tree Press • SolutionTree.com
Visit **go.SolutionTree.com/PLCbooks** to download this free reproducible.

Five Fundamental Resources
Extending Learning When Students Are Already Proficient

Tool: Extension Plan for a Unit of Study

Instructions: Use this template to plan extension opportunities for an upcoming unit of study.

Name of Unit:	
Extension Questions	**Your Response**
Think about the *essential standards* that your learning team has identified for this unit of study. What would you expect students to know and be able to do if they were working beyond grade-level proficiency with these essential standards? What learning experiences can you create that will give students in need of extension the chance to demonstrate these higher levels of proficiency?	
Think about the standards in your curriculum that your learning team determined are *not essential* for students to master in this unit of study. Which of those standards would be worth introducing to students in need of extension? Are there standards that students in need of extension would find especially engaging—or that will introduce students in need of extension to unique aspects of your content area that they wouldn't otherwise be exposed to? Are there standards that would help reinforce core knowledge and skills that students in need of extension will rely on in later grade levels?	
Think about the standards *covered in the next grade level's curriculum.* Which standards have learning teams in the grade level above you identified as essential for every student to master? Are any of those standards connected to the outcomes that your learning team has identified as essential for this unit of study? How could you give students in need of extension the chance to work with those standards right now?	

Tool: Weekly Extension Planning Template

Instructions: Complete this extension planning template at the beginning of each collaborative meeting to clarify your plans for addressing the needs of the question 4 students your learning team serves.

Learning Team: _____ **Date:** _____

Essential Outcomes We Are Teaching This Week	Best Strategy for Extending These Outcomes (Check one.)
	☐ Demonstrating mastery at levels beyond grade-level proficiency
	☐ Studying nonessential curriculum
	☐ Studying above-grade-level curriculum
	☐ Studying a real-life example of these outcomes in action

Our Initial Plan for Extending These Outcomes:

Five Fundamental Resources
Extending Learning When Students Are Already Proficient

Tool: Using Proficiency Scales to Define Levels of Mastery

Task: _____

Step 1: Defining Essential Learning

Instructions: With your team, identify the essential learning in the middle column. Then, define content that is both simpler and more complex than your essential learning.

Content that is **simpler** than your essential learning	Learning that you have identified as **essential**	Content that is **more complex** than your essential learning

Step 2: Identifying Five Levels of Mastery

Instructions: As a team and using the following outline described by Robert J. Marzano (2010), design a five-point rubric for scoring that describes the evidence that teachers should see in student responses demonstrating different levels of mastery.

Levels of Mastery	Points Earned	Evidence of Mastery
Student demonstrates mastery of content and skills beyond grade-level expectations.	4	
Student demonstrates mastery of content and skills that meet grade-level expectations.	3	
Student demonstrates mastery of content and skills that are simpler than grade-level expectations.	2	
Student depends on help from the teacher to demonstrate partial mastery of content and skills.	1	
Student cannot master grade-level content and skills even with teacher support.	0	

Reference

Marzano, R. J. (2010). _Formative assessment and standards-based grading_. Bloomington, IN: Marzano Resources.

Sample 1: Using Proficiency Scales to Define Levels of Mastery—Social Studies

Task: Social Studies—Understanding the Impact of the Silk Road on the Eastern and Western Worlds

Step 1: Defining Essential Learning

Instructions: With your team, identify the essential learning in the middle column. Then, define content that is both simpler and more complex than your essential learning.

Content that is **simpler** than your essential learning.	Learning that you have identified as **essential**	Content that is **more complex** than your essential learning
I can describe what the Silk Road was.	I can explain the impact that the Silk Road had on the cultures of both the Eastern and Western worlds.	I can give additional examples of ways in which political, economic, cultural, and religious ideas have spread across the globe over time.

Step 2: Identifying Five Levels of Mastery

Instructions: As a team and using the following outline described by Robert J. Marzano (2010), design a five-point rubric for scoring that describes the evidence that teachers should see in student responses demonstrating different levels of mastery.

Levels of Mastery	Points Earned	Evidence of Mastery
Student demonstrates mastery of content and skills beyond grade-level expectations.	4	☐ Student can analyze how different events throughout history resulted in the exchange of ideas that altered the economies, cultures, religions, and governments of different regions of the world. ☐ **Possible examples:** The salt trade of West Africa, the Crusades, colonization, World War II, the invention and widespread adoption of the internet, the global refugee crisis
Student demonstrates mastery of content and skills that meet grade-level expectations.	3	☐ Student correctly identifies the Silk Road as a series of trade routes that connected the Eastern and Western worlds during ancient times. ☐ Student understands that in addition to having an impact on the economies of the Eastern and the Western worlds, the exchange of ideas along the Silk Road had an impact on the religions, politics, and cultures of both regions. ☐ Student accurately names three different ideas that were introduced to the East and to the West by traders who traveled on the Silk Road and can rank them in importance from "having the greatest impact" to "having the least impact."

page 1 of 2

The Big Book of Tools for Collaborative Teams in a PLC at Work © 2020 Solution Tree Press • SolutionTree.com

Visit **go.SolutionTree.com/PLCbooks/BBTCT** and enter the unique access code found on the book's inside front cover to access this reproducible.

Five Fundamental Resources
Extending Learning When Students Are Already Proficient

Levels of Mastery	Points Earned	Evidence of Mastery
Student demonstrates mastery of content and skills that are simpler than grade-level expectations.	2	☐ Student correctly identifies the Silk Road as a series of trade routes that connected the Eastern and the Western worlds during ancient times. ☐ Student also explains how the Silk Road had a positive impact on the economies of the Eastern and Western worlds. ☐ Student does not, however, identify impacts that the Silk Road had on the politics, religions, or cultures of the Eastern and Western worlds.
Student depends on help from the teacher to demonstrate partial mastery of content and skills.	1	☐ Student correctly identifies the Silk Road as a series of trade routes that connected the East and the West during ancient times. ☐ Student does not, however, name any specific examples of the impact that these trade routes had on the Eastern and Western worlds.
Student cannot master grade-level content and skills even with teacher support.	0	☐ Student does not correctly identify the time period, general location, or overall purpose of the Silk Road.

Reference

Marzano, R. J. (2010). *Formative assessment and standards-based grading*. Bloomington, IN: Marzano Resources.

Sample 2: Using Proficiency Scales to Define Levels of Mastery—Physical Education

Task: Physical Education—Making a Layup in a Basketball Unit

Step 1: Defining Essential Learning

Instructions: With your team, identify the essential learning in the middle column. Then, define content that is both simpler and more complex than your essential learning.

Skills that are **simpler** than your essential learning	Learning that you have identified as **essential**	Skills that are **more complex** than your essential learning
I can score a basket from the standing position under the basket by jumping with two feet and then bouncing the ball off the backboard.	I can score a basket by making a layup during the flow of a game.	I can score a basket by making a layup outside the context of a game with either hand or from either side of the goal that I am attacking.

Step 2: Identifying Five Levels of Mastery

Instructions: As a team and using the following outline described by Robert J. Marzano (2010), design a five-point rubric for scoring that describes the evidence that teachers should see in student responses demonstrating different levels of mastery.

Levels of Mastery	Points Earned	Evidence of Mastery
Student demonstrates mastery of content and skills beyond grade-level expectations.	4	*Working independently, outside the context of a game and without defenders:* ☐ Student can make a layup with his or her nondominant hand. ☐ Student can rotate ball-side hand inward on release to add spin to the shot. ☐ Student can reverse the layup while under the basket, scoring from the opposite side of the original approach to the goal.
Student demonstrates mastery of content and skills that meet grade-level expectations.	3	*During a game:* ☐ Student can jump, leading with the leg on the ball side of the body. ☐ Student can move the knee and the elbow on the ball side of the body together and in the same direction. ☐ Student can fully extend ball-side arm toward the backboard. ☐ Student keeps ball-side hand with the palm facing inward.

Five Fundamental Resources
Extending Learning When Students Are Already Proficient

page 1 of 2

The Big Book of Tools for Collaborative Teams in a PLC at Work © 2020 Solution Tree Press • SolutionTree.com
Visit **go.SolutionTree.com/PLCbooks/BBTCT** and enter the unique access code found on the book's inside front cover to access this reproducible.

Levels of Mastery	Points Earned	Evidence of Mastery
Student demonstrates mastery of content and skills that are simpler than grade-level expectations.	2	*Working independently, outside of a game and without defenders:* ☐ Student can jump, leading with the leg on the ball side of the body. ☐ Student can move the knee and the elbow on the ball side of the body together and in the same direction. ☐ Student can fully extend ball-side arm toward the backboard. ☐ Student keeps ball-side hand with the palm facing inward.
Student depends on help from the teacher to demonstrate partial mastery of content and skills.	1	☐ Student can successfully score a basket by jumping with both feet and bouncing the ball off the backboard from a standing position under the basket. ☐ Student cannot, however, jump off one leg or use one hand while working with the basketball.
Student cannot master grade-level content and skills even with teacher support.	0	☐ Student cannot score a basket by jumping with both feet from a standing position under the basket.

Reference

Marzano, R. J. (2010). *Formative assessment and standards-based grading*. Bloomington, IN: Marzano Resources.

Key: Using Depth of Knowledge Levels to Increase the Complexity of an Existing Task

Instructions: One of the easiest ways to create extensions for question 4 students is to ask them to demonstrate mastery of essentials at levels that go beyond grade-level proficiency. Use this key, which outlines Norman L. Webb's (1997, 2002) Depth of Knowledge (DOK) levels, to increase the cognitive complexity of the tasks that you are already using as demonstrations of proficiency. You can then use those revised tasks as extensions for students who are ready to move beyond grade-level essentials.

Depth of Knowledge Key

DOK 1	DOK 2	DOK 3	DOK 4
Recall and Reproduction	**Skills and Concepts**	**Strategic Thinking**	**Extended Thinking**
DOK 1 tasks involve the simple recall of information. Answers to DOK 1 tasks are either right or wrong. No reasoning is required to complete DOK 1 tasks. Instead, students are gathering facts and information or applying simple formulas.	DOK 2 tasks involve the application of knowledge. Students explain, describe, categorize, or interpret information that they have acquired. DOK 2 tasks always require students to make decisions about how to approach problems.	DOK 3 tasks involve higher levels of reasoning than either of the two previous types of tasks. Students are asked to develop logical arguments based on evidence, to draw conclusions based on data, or to provide justifications and reasoning to defend their positions.	DOK 4 tasks involve the highest level of cognitive demands. Students are asked to make connections within or between content areas, to evaluate several possible solutions, or to explain alternative perspectives from multiple sources. DOK 4 tasks may also ask students to apply what they have learned to real-life contexts.
Sample task: Can you list the four main types of pathogens that cause diseases in humans?	**Sample task:** What are the similarities and differences between the two main types of pathogens that cause diseases in humans: (1) viruses and (2) bacteria?	**Sample task:** Rank order the four main types of pathogens that cause diseases in humans in order from "most dangerous" to "least dangerous." Defend your rankings with reasoning.	**Sample task:** Find an example of a disease outbreak that has happened in the world. Research the reasons for the outbreak, and offer recommendations about how the outbreak should have been treated.

Source: Definitions adapted from Webb, 2002.

References

Webb, N. L. (1997). *Research monograph number 6: Criteria for alignment of expectations and assessments in mathematics and science education*. Washington, DC: Council of Chief State School Officers.

Webb, N. L. (2002, March 28). *Depth-of-Knowledge levels for four content areas*. Accessed at http://facstaff.wcer.wisc.edu /normw/All%20content%20areas%20%20DOK%20levels%2032802.pdf on January 4, 2020.

Five Fundamental Resources: Extending Learning When Students Are Already Proficient

The Big Book of Tools for Collaborative Teams in a PLC at Work © 2020 Solution Tree Press • SolutionTree.com

Visit **go.SolutionTree.com/PLCbooks/BBTCT** and enter the unique access code found on the book's inside front cover to access this reproducible.

Tool: Using Depth of Knowledge Levels to Increase the Complexity of an Existing Task

Instructions: In the first column, write a short description of the task that students will complete to demonstrate proficiency with the grade-level essential that you are currently studying in class. List any materials that students will use while working on this task. Use the Depth of Knowledge (Webb, 2002) key on page 203 to increase the cognitive complexity of your current task. Then, in the second column, write a short description of the new, more complex task that you have created. List any materials that students will use while working on this task.

Essential Outcome We Are Studying:

Current Task	Extension Task

DOK Level of Current Task	DOK Level of Extension Task
☐ DOK 1: Recall and Reproduction	☐ DOK 1: Recall and Reproduction
☐ DOK 2: Skills and Concepts	☐ DOK 2: Skills and Concepts
☐ DOK 3: Strategic Thinking	☐ DOK 3: Strategic Thinking
☐ DOK 4: Extended Thinking	☐ DOK 4: Extended Thinking

Reference

Webb, N. L. (2002, March 28). *Depth-of-Knowledge levels for four content areas*. Accessed at http://facstaff.wcer.wisc.edu /normw/All%20content%20areas%20%20DOK%20levels%2032802.pdf on January 4, 2020.

The Big Book of Tools for Collaborative Teams in a PLC at Work © 2020 Solution Tree Press • SolutionTree.com

Visit **go.SolutionTree.com/PLCbooks/BBTCT** and enter the unique access code found on the book's inside front cover to access this reproducible.

Additional Resources

for Extending Learning When

Students Are Already Proficient

Tool: Building Your Learning Team's Knowledge About Extensions

Instructions: Use this tool to build knowledge about the four most common extension strategies. Then, use the questions that follow to reflect on your team's current extension practices.

Common Extension Strategies

Asking students to demonstrate mastery at levels beyond grade-level proficiency	Giving students opportunities to study nonessential curriculum
In most cases, curricula for different content areas have been carefully spiraled, exposing students to similar concepts at increasing levels of complexity from year to year. Collaborative teams use these curricular spirals to create proficiency scales and rubrics that define multiple levels of mastery for each essential outcome. Then, they use these scales and rubrics to extend learning by asking question 4 students to demonstrate mastery at levels that go beyond grade-level proficiency.	When working together to answer the first critical question of learning in a PLC (What do we want our students to learn?), collaborative teams divide the outcomes in their required curriculum into two simple categories: (1) need to knows and (2) nice to knows. Need to knows become the grade-level essentials that teams work together to ensure that every student learns. Nice to knows are nonessential outcomes that question 4 students can be exposed to as part of extension tasks.
Teaching students above-grade-level curriculum	**Introducing students to real-life examples of essential outcomes in action**
Learning in most content areas is progressional. The concepts and skills that students are introduced to this year are designed to prepare them for success in the same content area next year. As a result, effective teachers spend time studying what it is that students *have already learned* and what it is that students *are going to learn next*. High-performing learning teams use this knowledge of learning progressions in their curriculum to create extension tasks, giving question 4 students chances to wrestle with above-grade-level concepts and skills.	Students of all ages have an inherent need to see value in the content and skills that they are being asked to master. Engagement, then, is dependent on ensuring that students have a clear sense of why their learning matters. Collaborative teams use this need for relevance to create extensions by introducing question 4 students to real-life examples of essential outcomes in action or by asking question 4 students to use the knowledge that they have learned to solve real-life problems.

Questions for Reflection

Which of these common extension strategies does your team use most frequently? Why?

Which of these common extension strategies does your team use least often? Why?

Which of these common extension strategies feels the most doable to you? Why?

What steps can your team take right now to integrate more meaningful opportunities for extension into the work that you are doing with students?

Source: Adapted from DuFour, R., DuFour, R., Eaker, R., Many, T. W., & Mattos, M. (2016). Learning by doing: A handbook for Professional Learning Communities at Work *(3rd ed.). Bloomington, IN: Solution Tree Press; Roberts, M. (2019).* Enriching the learning: Meaningful extensions for proficient students in a PLC at Work. *Bloomington, IN: Solution Tree Press.*

Tool: Developing a Tiered Lesson Plan

Instructions: Use this template to begin planning a tiered lesson for one of the concepts in your curriculum.

Step 1: Define Content and Skills to Be Covered

Identify the lesson you are planning, and fill in the standards, content, and skills you will cover, along with your current instructional practices.

Name of Lesson:	
Academic Standards Covered by Lesson:	
What should all students *know* by the end of this lesson?	What should all students *be able to do* by the end of this lesson?
How do you currently teach this concept to students?	

Step 2: Define Levels of Student Performance

Use the prompts and questions in the left column to formulate your answers on the right.

Describe students who are **approaching** grade-level expectations on these standards and who will need scaffolding and support before reaching mastery. What do they already know? What can they already do? **What basic knowledge and skill gaps will you have to address in order to move these students forward?**	
Describe students who will **meet** grade-level expectations on these standards without extensive support. What do they already know? What can they already do? **How does that preexisting knowledge prepare these students to meet grade-level expectations?**	

Additional Resources
Extending Learning When Students Are Already Proficient

The Big Book of Tools for Collaborative Teams in a PLC at Work © 2020 Solution Tree Press • SolutionTree.com
Visit **go.SolutionTree.com/PLCbooks/BBTCT** and enter the unique access code found on the book's inside front cover to access this reproducible.

| Describe students who **exceed** grade-level expectations on these standards before teaching even begins. What do they already know? What can they already do?

What knowledge and skills are they ready to work with? | |

Step 3: Develop Leveled Activities for Students

When devising a **task** as part of a tiered lesson plan, think about what activity you can use to move students at a particular level of performance forward. In coming up with an effective **assessment**, consider which questions you could ask or tasks you could assign that would best determine whether a student is ready to move on to the next level of performance.

Level	Task	Assessment
Approaching Students in need of scaffolding and support in order to meet grade-level expectations; students missing foundational knowledge and skills necessary to meet grade-level expectations		
Meeting Students who meet grade-level expectations without needing extensive scaffolding or support; students who possess all the foundational knowledge and skills necessary to meet grade-level expectations		
Exceeding Students who are already working beyond grade-level expectations; students who need additional challenge or extension		

The Big Book of Tools for Collaborative Teams in a PLC at Work © 2020 Solution Tree Press • SolutionTree.com
Visit **go.SolutionTree.com/PLCbooks/BBTCT** and enter the unique access code found on the book's inside front cover to access this reproducible.

Step 4: Consider Planning Questions

Use the prompts and questions in the left column to formulate your answers on the right.

How will you determine the initial performance levels of all the students in your classroom? Will you use a pretest of some kind? Do you have any universal screening data that can help with initial placements? Can you use student work samples from previous assignments?	
How will you organize materials for each of your tiered activities? Will you store materials in individual stations around your room? Will you color code materials to represent individual levels of performance? Will you organize them into specific folders on your classroom website?	
How will you give directions and monitor progress while students are working on tiered activities? Will you develop a set of written directions for each level of performance? Will you use digital tools to record directions? Will you meet with individual groups on the day that tiered activities begin? Have you developed checkpoint tasks that you can use to determine student readiness to move forward? Do you have specific dates for delivering assessments to students? Will you meet with each student group every day to assess progress?	

Additional Resources
Extending Learning When Students Are Already Proficient

page 3 of 3

Tool: Developing a Tiered Task Card

Instructions: Use this template to create a tiered task card for an upcoming essential outcome. Start by listing the essential outcome that your students will learn. Then, develop three separate tasks that students could complete as demonstrations of mastery: one task for students who are approaching grade-level expectations, one task for students who are meeting grade-level expectations, and one task for students who are exceeding grade-level expectations. Finally, share this card with students and encourage them to use it as an anchor activity during regular classroom instruction.

Essential Outcome We Are Currently Learning:

Task That Students Approaching Grade-Level Expectations Should Be Able to Complete	Task That Students Meeting Grade-Level Expectations Should Be Able to Complete	Task That Students Exceeding Grade-Level Expectations Should Be Able to Complete

Questions for Reflection

What level of mastery are you currently working at?

What work products have you created that can serve as evidence of your current level of mastery?

What task are you going to tackle next?

Sample: Tiered Task Card—Elementary School Reading

Instructions: Use this template to create a tiered task card for an upcoming essential outcome. Start by listing the essential outcome that your students will learn. Then, develop three separate tasks that students could complete as demonstrations of mastery: one task for students who are approaching grade-level expectations, one task for students who are meeting grade-level expectations, and one task for students who are exceeding grade-level expectations. Finally, share this card with students and encourage them to use it as an anchor activity during regular classroom instruction.

Essential Outcome We Are Currently Learning: I can describe the characters in a story.		
Task That Students Approaching Grade-Level Expectations Should Be Able to Complete	**Task That Students Meeting Grade-Level Expectations Should Be Able to Complete**	**Task That Students Exceeding Grade-Level Expectations Should Be Able to Complete**
I can list details about each of the main characters in a story that I have read.	I can describe how the characters in a story that I have read respond to the major events and challenges that they face.	I can use evidence from a story that I have read to draw conclusions about the personalities of all the main characters.

Questions for Reflection

What level of mastery are you currently working at?

What work products have you created that can serve as evidence of your current level of mastery?

What task are you going to tackle next?

Tool: Curriculum Compacting Contract

Student Name: _____

Congratulations! Evidence shows that you have already mastered the outcomes that we are studying in class over the next few weeks. As a result, I would like to give you the opportunity to work at your own pace on extension tasks that go beyond our grade-level expectations. Please review the information on this contract, decide if this is an opportunity that you are interested in, and return the contract with both your signature and the signature of your parent or guardian.

Grade-Level Essentials We Are Studying	Evidence That You Are Already Proficient With These Grade-Level Essentials
(Directions for teachers: In student-friendly language, list the essential outcomes that you believe this student has already mastered.)	(Directions for teachers: List the evidence used to identify this student as a candidate for curriculum compacting. This may include pretest results, results on classroom tasks, and observational evidence.)
Tasks That You Must Complete to Guarantee Proficiency With Our Grade-Level Essentials	**Tasks That You Can Complete That Go Beyond Grade-Level Expectations**
(Directions for teachers: List two or three tasks that students must complete to prove that they really have mastered grade-level essentials.)	(Directions for teachers: List two or three extension tasks that students will work on independently during regular instruction time.)

I am interested in working at my own pace on extension tasks during the next few weeks of study. I understand that I will work on these tasks during regular instruction time and that my teacher will use the work products that I create to assess my level of mastery. I also understand that it is up to me to ask for help whenever I am stuck on an assignment.

Student Signature: _____   **Parent Signature:** _____

Sample: Curriculum Compacting Contract— Eighth-Grade Science

Student Name: _____

Congratulations! Evidence shows that you have already mastered the outcomes that we are studying in class over the next few weeks. As a result, I would like to give you the opportunity to work at your own pace on extension tasks that go beyond our grade-level expectations. Please review the information on this contract, decide if this is an opportunity that you are interested in, and return the contract with both your signature and the signature of your parent or guardian.

Grade-Level Essentials We Are Studying	Evidence That You Are Already Proficient With These Grade-Level Essentials
I can explain where water is found on Earth. I can explain the effect that the oceans have on living things. I can describe the characteristics of a healthy body of water.	Your unit pretest score: 93 The only questions missed were questions connected to the unique role that the properties of water play in keeping water healthy.
Tasks That You Must Complete to Guarantee Proficiency With Our Grade-Level Essentials	**Tasks That You Can Complete That Go Beyond Grade-Level Expectations**
Task 1: You must complete the Edpuzzle review video on properties of water and score a 100 on the review questions embedded in the video. **Task 2:** You must complete the fill-in-the-blank note sheet that goes along with the water properties slides that are posted in Google Classroom.	**Task 1:** When you were in sixth grade, you learned that water is one of the key elements that scientists look for when trying to identify planets that are suitable for supporting life. Why? What is it that makes water such an important ingredient for supporting life? Research an answer and develop a plan for sharing what you have learned with our class. **Task 2:** During our Drop in the Bucket lab, you learned that the amount of fresh water available on Earth is actually quite small. Is this a cause for concern? Are there areas on Earth that are running out of fresh water? What about our state? Is access to fresh water a concern? Research an answer and develop a plan for sharing what you have learned with our class.

I am interested in working at my own pace on extension tasks during the next few weeks of study. I understand that I will work on these tasks during regular instruction time and that my teacher will use the work products that I create to assess my level of mastery. I also understand that it is up to me to ask for help whenever I am stuck on an assignment.

Student Signature: _____   **Parent Signature:** _____

Additional Resources
Extending Learning When Students Are Already Proficient

Tool: Creating a Review Tutorial for an Essential Standard

Student Name: _____

Instructions: You have demonstrated mastery of the essential outcomes that we are studying in class. Now, it is time to see if you can teach those concepts to other people. Follow the steps to create a review tutorial that can be a great learning tool for your friends who are still trying to master the content that we are studying in class.

Learning Target That You Have Already Mastered:

Step 1: Think carefully about the objective.

What were the most important details to remember about this learning target? What were the least important details to remember about this learning target? What were the hardest things to understand about this learning target?

Step 2: Search for a video.

Using what you know about the learning target that you have already mastered, search for a video that introduces the important concepts and vocabulary in a way that other students would find engaging. Include a link to the video here. Then, evaluate the video in three categories: (1) content, (2) vocabulary, and (3) engagement.

Link to video:

Content	Vocabulary	Engagement
Essential content covered in this video:	Essential vocabulary defined in this video:	On a scale of 1 to 5, rate how engaging your peers will find this video:
Essential content missing from this video:	Essential vocabulary missing from this video:	Defend your rating with specific examples:

Step 3: Make a recommendation.

Would you recommend using this video in a review tutorial for students who are struggling with this learning target? Why or why not?

Step 4: Generate questions.

Write three questions that can be included in a review tutorial using this video. Remember that the questions you write should be designed to review the most important concepts and vocabulary related to the learning target that you have mastered.

Question	Minute Marker	Answers
	Where in the review tutorial should this question be included?	If you've written a multiple-choice question, include three options for answers and indicate the correct answer. If you've written an open-ended question, include a correct answer.

Once you have completed this form, share it with your teacher. After the video that you have selected and the questions that you have written have been approved, your teacher will help you use an online service like Edpuzzle (https://edpuzzle.com) to create your final product.

page 2 of 2

The Big Book of Tools for Collaborative Teams in a PLC at Work © 2020 Solution Tree Press • SolutionTree.com

Additional Resources

Extending Learning When Students Are Already Proficient

Tool: Using Student Wonder Questions as Extension Tasks

Student Name: _____

Instructions: Over the course of our next unit of study, your mind is going to be filled with interesting questions that we won't always have the time to answer during our daily lessons. Use this template to record those wonder questions. Then, after you have mastered the essential outcomes we are studying together in class, you can come back and answer them.

Topic Write down one or two words that best describe the topic of this wonder question.	Here's What I'm Wondering About Now, write down your wonder question. Remember to include as much detail as you can so that you have a good starting point for additional research when you go back to answer this question.	Here's What I Have Learned Finally, record anything new that you learn about your wonder question in this column. Consider including links to sources that you use so that you can continue to study more in the future.
Sample: Figurative language	*Sample:* I wonder if the tools of figurative language—things like similes and metaphors and personification—are used in speeches by presidents. I know that fiction writers use them all the time, but what about nonfiction writers?	*Sample:* Holy smokes—presidents use figurative language all the time! My favorite example is Theodore Roosevelt's (1910) "Man in the Arena" speech. In it, he says that "the poorest way to face life is to face it with a sneer." That is a neat way to describe a bad attitude.

The Big Book of Tools for Collaborative Teams in a PLC at Work © 2020 Solution Tree Press • SolutionTree.com
Visit **go.SolutionTree.com/PLCbooks/BBTCT** and enter the unique access code found on the book's inside front cover to access this reproducible.

Questions for Reflection

Do you see any patterns in the topics that you wonder about the most?

While researching answers to your wonder questions, did you discover any new topics worth studying or have any new wonder questions worth asking?

While researching, did you discover any new sources—websites, videos, books, people—that you would like to explore some more?

What connections can you make between the things that you learned while researching your wonder questions on your own and the content that we have been studying together in class?

Who would be interested in learning more about the wonder questions that you asked and the answers that you have found? Why?

Reference

Roosevelt, T. (1910). *Citizenship in a republic*. Speech given at the Sorbonne, Paris, France.

Tool: Tracking Real-Life Examples of Essential Outcomes in Action

Instructions: Each time that you see a news story or a video that models one of your essential outcomes in action, add it to this list. Then, write a short summary of the news story or video, describe how it is connected to your essential outcomes, and brainstorm an extension task that can be completed by students who are already proficient with the content that you are teaching in class.

Name of Unit of Study: _____

Link to News Story	Summary of News Story	Connection to Essential Outcomes	Task Question 4 Students Can Be Asked to Complete
Sample: "Water Crisis Puts Oregon Community at a Crossroads" www.npr.org/2020/01/01 /792692254/water-crisis-puts -oregon-community-at-a-crossroads	*Sample:* Because of heavy water use by farmers, aquifers relied on for drinking water are drying up in this rural Oregon community. That is creating tension between long-time residents and farmers, who both rely on the water.	*Sample:* We study the role that aquifers play in the storing of fresh water on Earth—and the way that water in aquifers is used by humans.	*Sample:* Based on what you have learned about aquifers, how concerned do you think residents should be about their current water crisis? Write a letter to the residents spotlighted in the article that articulates your position.

Questions for Reflection

Which of these extension opportunities was the most effective? Why?

Which of these extension opportunities was the least effective? Why?

How can you give more of your students opportunities to interact with the content covered in these extension opportunities?

Additional Resources
Extending Learning When Students Are Already Proficient

The Big Book of Tools for Collaborative Teams in a PLC at Work © 2020 Solution Tree Press • SolutionTree.com

Visit **go.SolutionTree.com/PLCbooks/BBTCT** and enter the unique access code found on the book's inside front cover to access this reproducible.

Tool: Rating the Extensions on Your Learning Team

Instructions: Complete one tracking template for each of the extension practices that your learning team experiments with. In a few short sentences, describe the extension. Then answer the questions in each column in order to fully outline the effectiveness of the extension, the materials you used, and ways to use this extension in the future. Finally, assign a rating to the extension using the provided scale.

Extension Practice

What essential knowledge and skills is this an extension of?

Evidence of Effectiveness	Required Materials	Future Revisions and Applications
How do you know that this extension was effective? What evidence have you collected to show that the extension has impacted student learning in a positive way? Did the extension work better for some students than others? Why?	What resources were necessary to ensure effective implementation of this extension? Include physical materials and lessons as well as any additional faculty members that helped with this extension practice.	What changes can you make to improve this extension practice moving forward?

Rate This Extension Practice

1	2	3	4	5
This extension was ineffective or difficult to implement. It isn't useful to our team and should be abandoned.	Despite showing signs of some promise, there are too many implementation challenges to make this extension worthwhile.	This extension has promise, but it is going to need significant revisions to remain part of our team's extension plans.	This extension was highly effective, and with a few simple revisions, it will be easy to implement. We should continue to polish and improve it.	This extension was highly effective and easy to implement just as it is. We should find ways to adapt it to new situations.

Tool: How Is Your Learning Team Spending Your Collaborative Time?

Instructions: Work individually to complete the task listed in step 1. Then, during a regularly scheduled team meeting, compare your responses with your peers'. Use the reflection questions at the end of this template to start a conversation about the ways that your learning team spends its collaborative time.

Step 1

Working individually, complete the following task.

Without exceeding 100 percent for the four critical questions, what percentage of your team's time do you spend in each of the following areas?	
Critical Question	**Percentage of Our Team's Time Spent on This Question**
What do we want all students to know and be able to do? Answering this question includes tasks like: • Identifying need to knows and nice to knows in our required curriculum • Deconstructing essential outcomes into learning targets • Rewriting learning targets in student-friendly language	
How will we know if they learn it? Answering this question includes tasks like: • Developing common formative assessments for each essential outcome • Developing proficiency scales or rubrics for grading subjective tasks • Organizing, analyzing, and reflecting on student learning data	
How will we respond when some students don't learn? Answering this question includes tasks like: • Developing additional practice activities for students struggling to master grade-level essentials • Preparing interventions for students who are struggling with work behaviors instead of academics • Dividing students into intervention groups that are targeted by need	
How will we extend learning for students who are already proficient? Answering this question includes tasks like: • Developing extension activities for students who have already mastered grade-level extensions • Using DOK levels to increase the cognitive complexity of existing assignments • Maintaining lists of real-life events that show examples of grade-level essentials in action	

Additional Resources Extending Learning When Students Are Already Proficient

page 1 of 2

Step 2

Working with your learning team, answer the following reflection questions.

Questions	Your Response
Which critical question does your learning team spend the most time answering?	
Which critical question does your learning team spend the least amount of time answering?	
What explains these patterns in the way that your learning team spends your collaborative time?	
What implications do these patterns in the way that your team spends your collaborative time have for students?	
What changes does your team need to make in order to ensure higher levels of learning for all students?	

Source: Adapted from Weichel, M., McCann, B., & Williams, T. (2018). When they already know it: How to extend and personalize student learning in a PLC at Work. Bloomington, IN: Solution Tree Press.

Checklist: Evaluating Your Team's Extension Practices

Instructions: Using the following key, circle your rating for each indicator. Then record your next steps in the last column.

Rating Key

1 = We haven't tackled this yet.
2 = We are developing or refining our work in this area.
3 = This is an established practice for our team.

Your Rating			Key Indicator	Next Steps
1	2	3	Our team believes that providing extensions to question 4 students is just as important as providing interventions to question 3 students.	
1	2	3	Our team has built-in time during every collaborative meeting for conversations about extending learning.	
1	2	3	Our team has worked together to identify the level of rigor expected in each of our grade-level essentials.	
1	2	3	Our team uses proficiency scales to define different levels of mastery for each of our grade-level essentials.	
1	2	3	Our team has a clear understanding of the four most common strategies used to extend learning for students.	
1	2	3	Our team "teaches up" by planning for extension first.	

Additional Resources

Extending Learning When Students Are Already Proficient

Your Rating			Key Indicator	Next Steps
1	2	3	Our team maintains lists of potential extensions for each of our grade-level essentials.	
1	2	3	Our team uses evidence of mastery of grade-level essentials—instead of gifted and talented labels, scholastic aptitude tests, or end-of-grade testing results—to identify students in need of extension.	
1	2	3	The extension tasks that our team develops require students to work thoughtfully at deep cognitive levels.	
1	2	3	Our team creates easy extensions by using Depth of Knowledge levels to increase the cognitive complexity of the tasks that we are already using as assessments of proficiency.	
1	2	3	Our team maintains a list of extension strategies and practices that we know have a positive impact on student learning.	
1	2	3	The extension tasks that our team uses are easy to implement.	

Additional Resources
Extending Learning When Students Are Already Proficient

The Big Book of Tools for Collaborative Teams in a PLC at Work © 2020 Solution Tree Press • SolutionTree.com
Visit **go.SolutionTree.com/PLCbooks/BBTCT** and enter the unique access code found on the book's inside front cover to access this reproducible.

Afterword

Let me finish with a simple statement: nothing has had a greater impact on who I am as an educator than the time that I have spent working in a professional learning community. I am energized by the work that I do with my collaborative peers. Together, we study practice—and that shared study of practice has made me a better teacher in almost every way. More importantly, that shared study of practice leaves me excited to head into work each morning because I know that I am going to learn something new from one of my peers that I can use to help more of my students learn at higher levels. I'm not intimidated by the increasingly diverse classrooms that I work in because I know that I'm never working alone. Instead, I'm surrounded by incredibly bright, incredibly talented people who are willing to learn alongside me. Together, there's no challenge that we can't tackle.

But I can't say that the work we do together has always been easy. We have had to learn a lot about what meaningful collaboration looks like in action. Early on, we figured out what norms were—and why they were so important to the effective functioning of a collaborative team. We also developed a better understanding of the kinds of tasks that teachers tackled when they were working through cycles of inquiry with one another. We learned how to choose essential outcomes, deconstruct standards, and identify common misconceptions. We started creating common assessments that were shorter, making it easier for us to learn from the data that we were collecting. And we made systematic plans to provide support to struggling learners and extensions to students who were already proficient. While we will always continue to polish our collaborative practices, our commitment to continuing to better understand the PLC process has left us in the place where we have a ton of expertise to offer.

That's why I wrote this book.

I want *you* to be as energized by the learning that you do with your peers as I am. I want you to recognize that there's nothing better—for you or for your students— than working in a high-performing professional learning community. And I want to share with you the tools that I have created and used over the years to keep my teams focused on the right work. I promise that if you give them a chance—use them to provide more explicit structure to the work that you are already doing with your peers—you will grow exponentially as a team.

References and Resources

Ainsworth, L. (2003). *"Unwrapping" the standards: A simple process to make standards manageable.* Englewood, CO: Advanced Learning Press.

Ainsworth, L., & Viegut, D. (2006). *Common formative assessments: How to connect standards-based instruction and assessment.* Thousand Oaks, CA: Corwin Press.

Bailey, K., & Jakicic, C. (2012). *Common formative assessment: A toolkit for Professional Learning Communities at Work.* Bloomington, IN: Solution Tree Press.

Bailey, K., & Jakicic, C. (2017). *Simplifying common assessment: A guide for Professional Learning Communities at Work.* Bloomington, IN: Solution Tree Press.

Bailey, K., & Jakicic, C. (2019). *Make it happen: Coaching with the four critical questions of PLCs at Work.* Bloomington, IN: Solution Tree Press.

Barth, R. S. (2006). Improving relationships within the schoolhouse. *Educational Leadership, 63*(6), 8–13.

Bloom, B. S. (Ed.). (1956). *Taxonomy of educational objectives, handbook I: Cognitive domain.* New York: Longman.

Buffum, A., & Mattos, M. (2020). *RTI at Work plan book.* Bloomington, IN: Solution Tree Press.

Buffum, A., Mattos, M., & Malone, J. (2018). *Taking action: A handbook for RTI at Work.* Bloomington, IN: Solution Tree Press.

Buffum, A., Mattos, M., & Weber, C. (2012). *Simplifying response to intervention: Four essential guiding principles.* Bloomington, IN: Solution Tree Press.

Canady, R. L. (2003, August). *Rethinking your grading practices.* Paper presented at the Wake County Public Schools Professional Learning Seminar, Raleigh, NC.

Conzemius, A. E., & O'Neill, J. (2014). *The handbook for SMART school teams: Revitalizing best practices for collaboration* (2nd ed.). Bloomington, IN: Solution Tree Press.

Dempsey, K. (2017, July 19). Does your school have a guaranteed and viable curriculum? How would you know? [Infographic]. *McREL International.* Accessed at https://mcrel.org/does-your-school-have-a-guaranteed-and-viable-curriculum on July 29, 2019.

Donohoo, J. (2017, January 9). *Collective teacher efficacy: The effect size research and six enabling conditions* [Blog post]. Accessed at https://thelearningexchange.ca/collective-teacher-efficacy on July 29, 2019.

DuFour, R. (2004). What is a professional learning community? *Educational Leadership, 61*(8), 6–11. Accessed at www.ascd.org/publications/educational-leadership/may04/vol61/num08/What-Is-a-Professional-Learning-Community%C2%A2.aspx on March 9, 2020.

DuFour, R., & DuFour, R. (2012). *The school leader's guide to Professional Learning Communities at Work*. Bloomington, IN: Solution Tree Press.

DuFour, R., DuFour, R., Eaker, R., Many, T. W., & Mattos, M. (2016). *Learning by doing: A handbook for Professional Learning Communities at Work* (3rd ed.). Bloomington, IN: Solution Tree Press.

European Parliament & Council of the European Union. (2006, December 18). *Recommendations of the European Parliament and the Council on key competencies for lifelong learning*. Accessed at http://eur-lex.europa.eu/legal-content/EN/ALL/?uri=celex %3A32006H0962 on January 22, 2020.

Fairfax County Public Schools Region 3 [FCPSR3]. (2017, October 31). *Kindergarten goal setting @MasonCrestES - never too early for students to own their progress! Thank you for sharing with @FCPSR3 today!* [Tweet]. Accessed at https://twitter.com/fcpsr3/status /925397646684184577 on January 27, 2020.

Ferriter, W. M. (2020, January 2). Extending learning in an #atplc school [Blog post]. *The Tempered Radical*. Accessed at https://blog.williamferriter.com/2020/01/02/extending -learning-in-an-atplc-school on February 14, 2020.

Ferriter, W. M., & Cancellieri, P. J. (2017). *Creating a culture of feedback*. Bloomington, IN: Solution Tree Press.

Ferriter, W. M., Graham, P., & Wight, M. (2013). *Making teamwork meaningful: Leading progress-driven collaboration in a PLC*. Bloomington, IN: Solution Tree Press.

Fisher, D., & Frey, N. (2012). Making time for feedback. *Educational Leadership*, *70*(1), 42–46.

Francis, E. (2017, May 9). *What is Depth of Knowledge?* [Blog post]. Accessed at https:// inservice.ascd.org/what-exactly-is-depth-of-knowledge-hint-its-not-a-wheel on January 4, 2020.

Graham, P., & Ferriter, W. M. (2008). One step at a time: Many professional learning teams pass through these seven stages. *Journal of Staff Development*, *29*(3), 38–42.

Graham, P., & Ferriter, W. M. (2010). *Building a Professional Learning Community at Work: A guide to the first year*. Bloomington, IN: Solution Tree Press.

Hattie, J. A. (n.d.). *What is "collective teacher efficacy"?* [Video file]. Accessed at https://vimeo .com/267382804 on July 29, 2019.

Hattie, J. A. (1992). Measuring the effects of schooling. *Australian Journal of Education*, *36*(1), 5–13.

Hattie, J. A. (2017). *Visible Learning Plus: 250+ influences on student achievement* [Infographic]. Accessed at https://visible-learning.org/wp-content/uploads/2018/03/VLPLUS-252 -Influences-Hattie-ranking-DEC-2017.pdf on July 29, 2019.

Hirsch, E. D., Jr. (1999). *The schools we need and why we don't have them*. New York: Anchor Books.

Jackson, Y. (2011). *The pedagogy of confidence: Inspiring high intellectual performance in urban schools*. New York: Teachers College Press.

Jacobs, H. H. (2001). New trends in curriculum: An interview with Heidi Hayes Jacobs. *Independent School*, *61*(1), 18–22.

Jakicic, C. (2018, October 2). *Formative assessments versus summative assessments* [Blog post]. Accessed at https://solutiontree.com/blog/formative-and-summative-assessment-differences on July 29, 2019.

Marzano, R. J. (2003). *What works in schools: Translating research into action.* Alexandria, VA: Association for Supervision and Curriculum Development.

Marzano, R. J. (2010). *Formative assessment and standards-based grading.* Bloomington, IN: Marzano Resources.

Marzano, R. J., Warrick, P. B., Rains, C. L., & DuFour, R. (2018). *Leading a high reliability school.* Bloomington, IN: Solution Tree Press.

National Commission on Excellence in Education. (1983). *A nation at risk: The imperative for educational reform.* Washington, DC: Author.

National Council for the Social Studies. (n.d.). *The college, career, and civic life (C3) framework for social studies state standards: Guidance for enhancing the rigor of K–12 civics, economics, geography, and history.* Accessed at www.socialstudies.org/sites/default/files/c3/C3-Framework-for-Social-Studies.pdf on October 7, 2019.

Partnership for 21st Century Learning. (2019). *Framework for 21st century learning.* Accessed at http://static.battelleforkids.org/documents/p21/P21_Framework_Brief.pdf on January 22, 2020.

Popham, W. J. (2003). *Test better, teach better: The instructional role of assessment.* Alexandria, VA: Association for Supervision and Curriculum Development.

Popham, W. J. (2008). *Transformative assessment.* Alexandria, VA: Association for Supervision and Curriculum Development.

Reeves, D. B. (2002). *The leader's guide to standards: A blueprint for educational equity and excellence.* San Francisco: Jossey-Bass.

Ritchhart, R., Church, M., & Morrison, K. (2011). *Making thinking visible: How to promote engagement, understanding, and independence for all learners.* San Francisco: Jossey-Bass.

Roberts, M. (2019). *Enriching the learning: Meaningful extensions for proficient students in a PLC at Work.* Bloomington, IN: Solution Tree Press.

Rockwell, D. (2017, March 16). *How to K.I.S.S. lousy operational meetings goodbye* [Blog post]. Accessed at https://leadershipfreak.blog/2017/03/16/how-to-k-i-s-s-lousy-operational-meetings-goodbye on August 5, 2019.

Roosevelt, T. (1910). *Citizenship in a republic.* Speech given at the Sorbonne, Paris, France.

Saphier, J. (2005). *John Adams' promise: How to have good schools for all our children, not just for some.* Acton, MA: Research for Better Teaching.

Smith, S. (2019, June 12). *How to be great? Just be good, repeatably* [Blog post]. Accessed at https://blog.stephsmith.io/how-to-be-great on August 9, 2019.

Sparks, S. K. (2008). Creating intentional collaboration. In C. Erkens, C. Jakicic, L. G. Jessie, D. King, S. V. Kramer, T. W. Many, et al., *The collaborative teacher: Working together as a professional learning community* (pp. 31–55). Bloomington, IN: Solution Tree Press.

Stiggins, R. J., Arter, J. A., Chappuis, J., & Chappuis, S. (2004). *Classroom assessment for student learning: Doing it right—using it well.* Portland, OR: Assessment Training Institute.

Stiggins, R. J., & Chappuis, J. (2005). Using student-involved classroom assessment to close achievement gaps. *Theory Into Practice, 44*(1), 11–18.

The Tarheelstate Teacher. (2015, December 6). *Multiplying with the area model error analysis* [Blog post]. Accessed at https://tarheelstateteacher.com/blog/multiplying-with-the-area -model-error-analysis on August 5, 2019.

Tomlinson, C. A. (2015, January 27). Differentiation does, in fact, work. *Education Week.* Accessed at www.edweek.org/ew/articles/2015/01/28/differentiation-does-in-fact-work. html on January 2, 2020.

Tomlinson, C. A. (2017). *How to differentiate instruction in academically diverse classrooms* (3rd ed.). Alexandria, VA: Association for Supervision and Curriculum Development.

Venables, D. R. (2011). *The practice of authentic PLCs: A guide to effective teacher teams.* Thousand Oaks, CA: Corwin Press.

Wagner, T. (2008). *The global achievement gap: Why even our best schools don't teach the new survival skills our children need—and what we can do about it.* New York: Basic Books.

Webb, N. L. (1997). *Research monograph number 6: Criteria for alignment of expectations and assessments in mathematics and science education.* Washington, DC: Council of Chief State School Officers.

Webb, N. L. (2002, March 28). *Depth-of-Knowledge levels for four content areas.* Accessed at http://facstaff.wcer.wisc.edu/normw/All%20content%20areas%20%20DOK%20 levels%2032802.pdf on January 4, 2020.

Weichel, M., McCann, B., & Williams, T. (2018). *When they already know it: How to extend and personalize student learning in a PLC at Work.* Bloomington, IN: Solution Tree Press.

Williams, K. C. (2016, August 17). *How to use common formative assessments to help teachers reflect on practice* [Video file]. Accessed at https://youtube.com/watch?v=9p3Fp5rBdz8 on August 5, 2019.

Index

Learning by Doing, 3rd Edition
Richard DuFour, Rebecca DuFour, Robert Eaker, Thomas W. Many, and Mike Mattos
Discover how to transform your school or district into a high-performing PLC. The third edition of this comprehensive action guide offers new strategies for addressing critical PLC topics, including hiring and retaining new staff, creating team-developed common formative assessments, and more.
BKF746

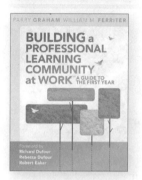

Building a Professional Learning Community at Work®
Parry Graham and William M. Ferriter
This play-by-play guide to implementing PLC concepts uses a story to focus each chapter. The authors analyze the story, highlighting good decisions and mistakes. They offer research behind best practice and wrap up each chapter with practical recommendations and tools.
BKF273

Creating a Culture of Feedback
William M. Ferriter and Paul J. Cancellieri
Because of the importance placed on high-stakes evaluations, schools have built up cultures that greatly emphasize grading. Discover how to shift your classroom focus to prioritize effective feedback over grades, giving students all the information they need to succeed.
BKF731

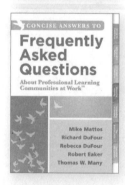

Concise Answers to Frequently Asked Questions About Professional Learning Communities at Work®
Mike Mattos, Richard DuFour, Rebecca DuFour, Robert Eaker, and Thomas W. Many
Get all of your PLC questions answered. Designed as a companion resource to *Learning by Doing: A Handbook for Professional Learning Communities at Work* (3rd ed.), this powerful, quick-reference guidebook is a must-have for teacher teams working to build and sustain a PLC.
BKF705

Help Your Team
Michael D. Bayewitz, Scott A. Cunningham, Joseph A. Ianora, Brandon Jones, Maria Nielsen, Will Remmert, Bob Sonju, and Jeanne Spiller
Written by eight PLC at Work® experts, this practical guide addresses the most common challenges facing collaborative teams. Each chapter offers a variety of templates, processes, and strategies to help your team resolve conflict, focus on the right work, and take collective responsibility for student success.
BKF886

Solution Tree | Press   *a division of* Solution Tree   Visit SolutionTree.com or call 800.733.6786 to order.

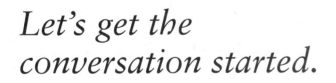